I0801348

HAS HOLLYWOOD
Lost its mind?

LES PG13
GUI PG13 6:0
HE G :PG 2:50
ING .PG 3:50
.R 3:00
PG13 4:45
TRIP PG13 3:40
.PG13 2:40
.PG13 4:00
R 3:00

HAS HOLLYWOOD *Lost its mind?*

A PARENT'S GUIDE TO MOVIE RATINGS

CHRIS HICKS

familius

Published by Familius LLC, www.familius.com

Familius books are available at special discounts for bulk purchases for sales promotions, family, or corporate use. Special editions, including personalized covers, excerpts of existing books, or books with corporate logos, can be created in large quantities for special needs. For more information, contact Premium Sales at 801-552-7298 or email specialmarkets@familius.com

Library of Congress Catalog-in-Publication Data
2012950691

pISBN 978-1-938301-19-3
eISBN 978-1-938301-20-9

Printed in the United States of America

Book design by Kurt Wahlner
Edited by Edith Songer

10 9 8 7 6 5 4 3 2 1

First Edition

Contents

For my long-suffering wife
Joyce, and my children,
stepchildren, and grandchil-
dren—not one of whom is
without a strong opinion,
and I treasure every debate.

Foreword

According to their adult leader, it was going to be a small scout troop, just nine teenage boys, all of them avid moviegoers and all of them excited about the opportunity to babble on about the latest releases. The subject would be movies in general and the rating system in particular, and the troop leader assured me they were all "good boys" who made it a rule to avoid R-rated movies. It was a subject he had discussed with them at length, he said, and he emphasized this a couple of times during our brief telephone conversation beforehand.

As the movie critic for two decades at the daily Salt Lake City newspaper the *Deseret News*, I was often asked to speak to high school and college classes, local service clubs, and various religious groups about movie ratings, especially in the 1980s and early '90s when my profile was raised by taking on movie "specialist" duties for KSL TV and radio for thirteen years. In other words, this was not my first rodeo, as the cliché goes, and I smiled at the troop leader's emphatic declaration that these boys never watched R-rated movies.

Since this was such a small gathering, we met at the scout leader's home, sitting on couches and soft chairs; it was one of the more intimate and informal settings I'd been invited to. The boys were genial and friendly, and they were indeed enthusiastic about movies. I started with some friendly, get-to-know-you humor, then laid out the rating system in understandable terms . . . or as understandable as the rating system can be . . . and after about twenty minutes, I opened it up to questions.

As is often the case with young people, the questions started out on topic but soon devolved into the usual "What did you think of this movie?" and "What about that movie?" as they named their favorites and challenged me to agree.

They were smart kids and it was fun—one of my more enjoyable outings of this kind. When the hour concluded, I said my goodbyes and the troop leader walked me to the door. As I started to step outside, when I could see that we were out of earshot of the young men, I leaned into the leader and said, "You're right, they are good boys. I enjoyed them very much." He smiled.

Then I added, "But you know, of course, that half the titles they threw at me, all those movies they had seen and were going on and on about, were R-rated movies." His face fell. "Really?" he said incredulously. "That's right," I said, "but don't be too hard on them. I suspect they never really look at the ratings. Especially when they watch movies on home video. After all, you didn't know they were R-rated either, right?"

This is not an atypical scenario. When young people are the audience, this is often how it goes. Hey, they're teenagers. They push things. I had teens at home for many years. And I was a teen once myself, I know how it goes. They're always looking to fit in, to look good, to avoid being ostracized, and above all, they don't want to seem like a goody-goody, as if they're saying they are better than their peers. Even if they're not inclined to watch a particular movie, they are still likely to go along with the crowd rather than rock the boat.

There were times when my kids were young, that I found out about things they had done or participated in that made me proud. But there were just as many times when information came my way that made me wince. The good news is that all of my children grew up to be responsible adults; they love and care for their own families, they all have good jobs, they contribute to society . . . they made it.

All parents know that there are hiccups along the way, and sometimes there are earthquakes. And now that some of my kids have kids of their own, they get it. Even those who don't have their own children observe their nieces and nephews and have come to understand the importance of trying to guide them toward responsible choices. And today, more than ever, that includes entertainment.

As a watchful, caretaker parent all those years, I had many crocodile-infested waters to navigate. When I started paying attention to movie ratings, both professionally and as a parent, I learned pretty quickly that Hollywood movers and shakers like to "push the envelope," as they put it, and it doesn't seem to matter whether it's a children's film or an adult movie. It's not just R-rated movies that are troubling. PG-13s are often more troubling. And even PGs can be problematic—sometimes worse than problematic. Simply put, relying on the Motion Picture Association of America to make choices for you or your children is a mistake.

A recent TV commercial has a young girl talking on the phone near her mother and father, and she's saying things openly that no kid would dream of verbalizing within hearing range of her folks. Naturally the parents react in a shocked manner as the announcer says something about "if kids talked at home the way they talk online . . ."

It's meant as a cautionary tale about how carried away youngsters become when they have too much freedom on the Internet, but there's an analogy here to the rating system. What if the family sat down together—Mom, Dad, young children, teens, perhaps even grandparents—and started watching a movie that began to display wall-to-wall foul language, casual sex, nudity, recreational drug use, and/or graphic violence? Would you stay with that show or turn it off? You'd probably either find something else to watch or pull a board game off the shelf. But often parents let their kids go to movies, or watch something at a friend's house, never suspecting that the film in question will be offensive.

I once suggested in a column that movies might be very different if filmmakers had their children—or their mothers or grandmothers—sitting next to them as they sat in the director's chair. When we're watching something with people we care about, in particular those who are young (with impressionable, still-forming minds), a censoring response kicks in that is quite different than when we watch things alone. That response should give us a clue about the kind of things children are seeing all the time.

The rating system is designed for parents, to help them guide their children, but it's imperfect, as you'll see.

I'm asked all the time, "What's the best way to know what our kids are being exposed to?" The best way, of course, is to see it yourself. But that is, at best, an impractical solution. There are lots of websites that offer blow-by-blow descriptions of every little potentially offensive element of modern movies, but even that can be a bit misleading, sometimes in the other direction. A movie with a strong positive message, showing characters dealing with life's hurdles, might be made to sound much worse than it is if you simply look at an out-of-context list of every crass word or gesture it contains.

Say, for example, you'd heard good things about a certain film and

William Edmunds, James Stewart and Stanley Andrews in a tense bar scene in Frank Capra's It's a Wonderful Life *(1946) —Liberty Films*

were thinking about renting it, so you decide to look at a list of its potentially offensive content and discover it has scenes depicting men and women smoking cigarettes and drinking alcohol, a naked woman hiding in the bushes, a man slapping a boy across the face, a boy nearly drowning in icy water, a man being punched by another man, a policeman firing a gun at an unarmed man, the protagonist getting drunk in a rowdy bar, another drunken man accidentally spiking a medicine bottle with poison, and a man attempting suicide by jumping off a bridge in a snowstorm . . .would you automatically say, "Forget it!" or would you decide to sit down with your kids and watch *It's a Wonderful Life* during the holidays as millions of families do each year?

Every story needs conflict. Every hero needs something to overcome. Every tale of positive growth requires a negative obstacle for the hero/heroine to go through first. With a specific list of "offenses," it's sometimes hard to remember that it's all in the telling. Some filmmakers offer up such things by implication, others show everything possible, and most fall somewhere in between. And it must be factored in that some audience members will be offended by certain things that don't really bother others.

So what's the answer? In the end, you really have to come up with your own. I hope the information here will offer some help—a guide, if you will, through some of the perils of the movie-watching swamp. I include suggestions for navigation, and, after you make your way through the quagmire, some good news: There are new movies out there that you might want to consider for family viewing. Some may have slipped past you; some you wanted to see but never got to; some you may have forgotten about. There are always good movies out there but sometimes it's difficult to find them without a little help.

Some of this material appeared in the *Deseret News* in the form of reviews, columns, and feature stories during my twenty years on the see-everything movie-reviewing beat, and my more than thirty years of writing a weekly entertainment column. And I would be remiss if I didn't thank the many editors and colleagues I've worked with over the years who have helped make sense of my scribblings, as well as the editors at Familius who have done the same here.

Introduction

"The more things change, the more they stay the same."

That's a rough translation of an epigram from mid-19th century French writer Jean-Baptiste Alphonse Karr which obviously has resonance in the 21st century. And it can be applied directly to the motion picture rating system.

More than 30 years ago, in June 1981, I wrote this *Deseret News* story about movie ratings, and it's still relevant. All you need to do is update the movie titles, keep in mind that the PG-13 rating was still three years away, and remember it would be another nine years before the X rating would be replaced by NC-17.

> The wire-thin line that separates movies rated PG and R has been crossed over so many times in both directions that industry observers are questioning whether the rating system carries any validity at all. A recent nationally syndicated Knight-Ridder article expressed dismay that a single rating can include both *Ordinary People* and *The Postman Always Rings Twice.* Both films are rated R.
>
> *Ordinary People,* which was a multiple Oscar-winner this year (1981), was rated R because of one particular profanity that automatically gets that rating. The word is used in an explosive, emotional pair of scenes, eight times in all, including once in a sexual context, but the film contains no nudity, no sex, no violence, and little other profanity.

The Postman Always Rings Twice has sexual scenes so explicit that the reviewer for Variety, the show business trade journal, wrote, "If this is an R, the only X left is actual hard core." It also was very violent, the dialogue was almost constant profanity, and there was nudity, albeit fleetingly.

There are also PG-rated movies that once were R-rated or look like they still should be.

The same profanity that brought *Ordinary People* an R was used about four times in *Inside Moves*, a Christmas release last year (1980). That film was originally rated R, but the director asked the rating board for a reduced rating. The board agreed and it received a PG without any cuts. One day an R the next a PG. *Inside Moves* also contains quite a lot of other profanity and some violence.

These following four films, however, did not have to fight for PG ratings, and every one could easily have been rated R; *The Competition*, with a love-making scene between an unmarried couple that leaves little to the imagination; *The Idolmaker*, which, though it does not use the R-rated profanity, does use nearly every other sex-related profanity imaginable; *Sphinx*, which opens with the graphic depiction of a man, with ropes tied from his arms and legs to four horses, literally being torn apart; *Tribute*, which has a subplot about a prostitute being honored by her past customers, and a scene where she disrobes before Jack Lemmon in his apartment.

To understand just how subjective the rating system is, it's important to realize that movies are rated by members of a board that is under the auspices of the movie industry.

The Classification and Rating Administration (CARA), which affixes the G, PG, R or X to movies released in the United States is under the direction of the Motion Picture Association of America (MPAA). It is composed of eight to eleven men and women who view movies and discuss them, casting votes to decide ratings. Its chairman, an MPAA employee, casts tie-breaking votes.

The criteria are simple: Movies are rated on the basis of content — violence, profanity, sex, nudity, vulgarity, theme — without regard to artistic quality or intent. The only firm rule concerns one sexually-based profanity that automatically gets an R; all else is on the basis of discussion and vote. Any film may be appealed, and if certain cuts are made, a rating may be reduced by the board. In some cases (as with *Inside Moves*, and a few years earlier with *All the President's Men*, *The Front*, and others), no changes are required, and a rating will still be reduced.

But the mind boggles at a system that puts a PG on the very violent *Lion of the Desert* and an R on the extremely

Jack Nicholson and Jessica Lange in the 1981 remake of The Postman Always Rings Twice —MGM

tame *Hopscotch*; or a PG on the very gruesome horror movie *Road Games* and an R on the light-hearted *The Blues Brothers*.

Perhaps, a closer-to-home example is the contrast between two films that are similar in theme. *Kramer vs. Kramer*, which has nudity, sex, and profanity, is rated PG; *Ordinary People*, with profanity only, is rated R.

It's been a gradual, creeping plague that has turned the rating system inside out. When films were first being rated, the criteria to distinguish a PG from an R were clearer. Then, one-by-one, certain films came along to challenge the system—a partially nude lovemaking scene in *Ryan's Daughter*, profanity in *Patton*, violence in *Jaws*—each with scenes that broke down barriers to help material that had never been allowed in PG-rated movies before suddenly become acceptable.

Nowadays, any profanity except the one sexually explicit word referred to previously—and sometimes even that—may be heard in a PG film. Is that word any worse than repeatedly taking the Lord's name in vain? Apparently, the rating board thinks so.

Meanwhile, G-rated films have become rare. The first year of the ratings, 1968, saw 141 G-rated movies, but the numbers have steadily decreased each year. Of 326 movies rated last year, only fifteen were rated G, and many of those were independent films, not major studio pictures.

The decline is due to a stigma that developed after a number of G movies failed to make money. The feeling spread that the rating implied to viewers that the films were too tame. (Some critics have suggested it is actually because those G movies were simply not good films.) So, producers decided to spice up their family fare by including language or "edgy" scenes to ensure a PG.

Of 326 movies rated last year, 129 were PG and 151 were R. In Salt Lake City this year, so far, thirty-nine PG-rated movies have been released, forty-eight R and only six rated G.

> Despite the fact that they are clean films intended for the family, and that most parents would allow their children to see them, *Superman II*, *Popeye*, *The Devil and Max Devlin*, *The Empire Strikes Back*, and *Little Miss Marker* all wound up with PG ratings instead of Gs—the same rating received by the very violent *Legend of the Lone Ranger* and the very raunchy *Airplane!*
>
> Though those directly connected with the rating system often assert that it works, and that families have gotten behind it, even CARA sees the weaknesses.
>
> Ratings have some value as a general guide, but they should not be relied on wholly. More education about each film is necessary. Reading reviews in various publications and talking to friends who have seen specific films are useful in learning what movies should be seen. Another way is for parents to see a film themselves before allowing their children to do so.

So what's changed since 1981? Not much, really. Today, ratings come with brief explanations, and there is a vast array of websites that can provide you with more specific details about movie content. But the only real change of substance is the titles.

In 2011, it was *The King's Speech* and *Win Win* that received R ratings for the use of a few f-words, which seemed extreme since it put those films in the same category as the year's really hard R-rated releases: *Bridesmaids*, *The Hangover - Part II*, *The Girl with the Dragon Tattoo*, *Scream 4*, *The Rum Diary*, *Horrible Bosses*, etc.

CARA is still run by the MPAA, ratings are still doled out by committee in the same manner, and many parents are still baffled by some of CARA's decisions. Of course, a lot of this also has to do with filmmakers who tend to try and get away with as much as they can and still acquire softer ratings for their films. My guess is that the board members who rate the films are also often confused.

Meanwhile, the G rating still seems to be in jeopardy, and now so does the PG. The NC-17, which replaced the X rating, is rarely used, with most filmmakers whose works receive an NC-17 opting for one of two alternatives: tone down the film with minor edits and appeal for an R rating, or leave the film as is and simply reject the rating. If the distribution agency is not a major studio, the film can go into theaters "Unrated" or "Not Rated," as often happens with independent productions.

As to where these films fall in terms of numbers, let's look at the national statistics for 2011. According to www.mpaa.org, the Motion Picture Association of America's website, the board gave ratings to 758 films in 2011, and the vast majority—589—were from sources other than the major studios. In other words, 589 of the movies that received ratings in 2011 were produced by independent filmmakers or were foreign films (although some were purchased for distribution by the major studios).

Kate Nowlin, Marley Shelton, and Carla Gugino in The Mighty Macs *(2011)*
—Sony

Some 600 movies were distributed to North American theaters in 2011—including 233 that went into release with no rating—but most cities around the United States saw fewer than half of those come through town. The vast majority of these films played briefly in major metropolitan movie houses and then went straight to home-video outlets.

With that in mind, here's a breakdown of 2011 movies that were rated, and which were available in your local movie theaters, according to Box Office Mojo (www.boxofficemojo.com) which tracks such things:

★ Fifteen new G-rated movies were released nationally. Six of them were animated features aimed at children and seven were documentaries. Only two G-rated live-action features for adult/family audiences were released in 2011, *Seven Days in Utopia* and *The Mighty Macs*, both of which are low-budget independent films with Christian themes. So, aside from cartoons and documentaries, the major studios did not release a single G-rated movie aimed at adults.

★ Forty-nine PG-rated movies found national distribution. Of those, nearly half played exclusively in major cities, never coming to theaters in medium-size or smaller venues around the country. Of the twenty-six that did play in theaters all over America, ten were cartoons, eight were for children or young teens, and another eight were designed for adult or family audiences: *The Muppets*, *We Bought a Zoo*, *Jack and Jill*, *Hugo*, *Dolphin Tale*, *Soul Surfer*, *Johnny English Reborn*, and *The Big Year*.

★ There were 129 PG-13 films released in 2011, and of those, 69 received distribution to theaters all around the country, ranging from franchise hits in the *Harry Potter*, *Transformers*, *Twilight*, and *Pirates of the Caribbean* series to films with very adult themes, such as *The Help*, *Just Go With It*, *Crazy, Stupid, Love*, *Contagion*, *Moneyball*, etc. Of the rest, many started out in large metropolitan areas, then trickled into towns around the country, playing primarily in art-film venues, including *The Tree of Life*, *Jane Eyre*, *A Separation*, *The Beaver*, etc. And some were rolled out even more slowly, such as *October Baby*, which started crisscrossing the country in October 2011 and was just getting to some smaller venues by spring 2012. Still others played a few major cities and fell off the map, going to home video or just disappearing.

★ The R rating continues to dominate, with 174 R-rated movies going into release in 2011. Of those, forty-three went into wide distribution, including *The Hangover - Part II*, *Bridesmaids*, *The Girl with the Dragon Tattoo*, *Final Destination 5*, *J. Edgar*, *My Weekend with Marilyn*, etc. Of the remaining 131, about half—including such popular films as *Win Win*, *Beginners*, *Company Men*, *Melancholia* and *Martha Marcy May Marlene*—started out in major metropolitan theaters and then spread around the country a few cities at a time. The other half played in metro areas and then went straight to DVD/Blu-ray, streaming sites, video-on-demand cable channels, or just faded away.

★ There was only one NC-17 movie released in 2011, *Shame*, which played in the big cities in December and then made its way through art houses around the country over the first couple of months in 2012.

The purpose of sharing these statistics is to impress upon the reader just how many movies come out every year, how many will likely come to your town, how many others you may have to thumb through the next time you open your Netflix account, and especially how many are seen by members of the movie-rating board. There must be some really bleary-eyed board members by the end of the week. No wonder they only serve two or three years.

I have attempted with this book to offer a clear-eyed exploration of the movie ratings, what they mean, and how they are administered. I also examine a variety of movies that carry the various ratings so as to provide concrete examples by using titles with which you may have at least a passing familiarity. Note: It is important for the reader to keep in mind that throughout most of these discussions the quality of the movies is irrelevant.

I may inject opinions here and there—and in the final chapter you will find many movies I am recommending—but for the most part, when I'm throwing out titles with cursory synopses, it is strictly to point out content and make comparisons with other films that are equally offensive or inoffensive. Therefore, a really terrible movie may be mentioned in the same breath with a good one, or even a great one, but that doesn't mean they are being compared by quality. Rather they are being compared strictly for content as it relates to the ratings.

It's a difficult enough thing to counteract the many negative influences our impressionable, pre-adolescent, "tween," and teenage children are exposed to these days without the rating system continually muddying things up. But then, none of us want Hollywood to decide what our children should see.

The ratings are not entirely without value, but they should be just a part of the process that helps us figure out what our children should be allowed to see. A rating is, perhaps, a first step. Most Gs and PGs are not so worrisome, but a film with a PG-13 definitely needs closer examination. There are many ways available these days to obtain more information about any movie that plays in any of the many venues, from theaters to DVD/Blu-ray to online accessibility.

Chapter 1

HOLLYWOOD CENSORS ITSELF

The voluntary movie rating system was born on November 1, 1968, the offspring of Jack Valenti, then head of the Motion Picture Association of America (MPAA). Valenti created the ratings as a way of deflecting government censorship, which had been hovering over the movie industry since the late 1950s, when those flickering images in theaters around the country suddenly began to say things and show things that for many years had been forbidden. Parents were in an uproar, school boards were calling for reforms, and newspapers were editorializing about our children being threatened by shocking depravities on the big screen that were far too adult for their tender minds to process.

Actually, this was nothing new. Movies had been offending audiences and prompting censorship by local government entities, almost since the first cinematic entertainment began popping up throughout the country at the turn of the 20th century. During that first decade of the 1900s, movie studios found themselves doing battle with state, county, city, and town censorship boards, which often banned certain movies outright or took the scissors to them, editing out the naughty bits.

As you might expect, this disturbed the moviemakers and did not sit well with the studios that distributed the films. It was like publishing books only to have local censorship boards tear out pages before allowing them to be placed in local libraries. So, the distributors—there were only three major studios at the time—decided to become as organized as the boards that challenged them.

In 1922, the Motion Picture Producers and Distributors of America (MPPDA) was formed and all of the burgeoning movie studios agreed to belong. They picked United States Postmaster General Will H. Hays to be the organization's president, luring him away from President Warren G. Harding's cabinet. Among Hays' duties was figuring out a way to help the movie industry self-regulate content, which, it was hoped, would alleviate the need for all those pesky, restrictive, blue-nosed boards.

It didn't take long for Hays to create the Studio Relations Committee (SRC), which pulled together all of the complaints from the boards around the country, evaluated them, and compiled a list of things to avoid in the movies so as not to traverse the boundaries of good taste. In 1927, a specific list of dos and (mostly) don'ts was published and circulated among studios, but it was largely ignored. Over the next couple of years, as nothing seemed to change, local boards continued to complain, ban, and snip away.

Also, in 1927, an experimental innovation revolutionized the industry almost overnight—the advent of sound, popularized in a half-silent/half sound picture titled *The Jazz Singer*, starring Al Jolson, a very well-known singing sensation whose incredible stage charisma translated comfortably to the big screen.

Though most of the film still used black-and-white printed intertitles for dialogue, a sequence about 15 minutes into the show caused a sensation when it was seen—and heard—by audiences for the first time. Jolson is sitting in a nightclub and is called up to sing a song, so he performs "Dirty Hands, Dirty Face," and the audience actually hears it. Then Jolson speaks, using his already famous catchphrase, "You ain't heard nothin' yet," and goes into one of his most popular songs, "Toot, Toot, Tootsie." The crowd went wild—both the audience in the movie and the movie audiences in the theaters.

Sound was not really new to the movies; short films had experimented with it since the early 1920s. But this was a full-length feature from a major studio (Warner Bros.) and its enormous popularity signaled the entrance of the "talkies" and the decline of the "silents." It also signaled a change for the SRC. No longer did the board just have to worry about what was shown on the screen. Now it also had to worry about what was said.

As a result, with religious groups campaigning for federal intervention, Hays took another step, and in 1930 made public a policy statement about cinematic content, which he called the Motion Picture Production Code. With the SRC, Hays created a sort of Ten (or so) Commandments for moviemakers. These "thou shalt nots" were designed to eliminate a lot of the same things that today's rating system only warns us about: graphic violence, sex, nudity, foul language, drug abuse, etc.

But there were a number of other specific things that the Production Code would also not allow to be shown, or, in some cases, even to be discussed: childbirth, interracial relations, ethnic slurs, ridicule of religion, cruelty toward children or animals, suggestive dancing, couples in bed together, surgical operations, detailed criminal activity, lustful kissing, prostitution, etc. And the range of disallowed words, aside from the expected profanities, included "alley cat," "tart," "pansy," and other slang terms of the period.

The trouble was, none of the studios, and certainly none of the filmmakers, seemed to care about the Code. As the silent era faded and the studios switched to sound productions in earnest, the Production Code was often ignored. In fact, a great many movies released during the Code's first four years of existence—many of them available on home video now—can be seen as obviously thumbing their noses at the restrictions.

Edward G. Robinson and James Cagney made their names with

stellar performances as ruthless gangsters in, respectively, *Little Caesar* (1930) and *The Public Enemy* (1931), both laced with bloody, violent crime and whose title characters are ultimately gunned down in the streets.

Gruesome images were the order of the day in the horror films *Freaks* (1932), with real-life deformed players in a story of love, hate, and revenge among circus folk (such exploitation of people with unusual birth defects was common among traveling sideshows of the era), and *Island of Lost Souls* (1933), an adaptation of H.G. Wells' *The Island of Dr. Moreau*, in which a mad scientist (Charles Laughton) creates half-man, half-beast creatures who revolt.

More familiar movie monsters also cropped up during this period, including the granddaddies of them all, *Frankenstein* and *Dracula*, both released in 1931, which became so popular that their respective stars, Boris Karloff and Bela Lugosi, remain recognizable icons to this day. By 21st century standards these films are, to say the least, quite tame in their representations of horror, but in 1931 both were quite controversial. A sequence in *Frankenstein* shows the monster accidentally killing a child, and *Dracula* mixes sex with violence.

Sex and violence also plagued *King Kong* in 1933, in particular a scene in which Kong peels the clothing off of scream-queen Fay Wray as if she were a banana. (These scenes in *Frankenstein* and *King Kong* were deleted from release prints after 1934 and were only restored in the 1980s when home video came into play.)

Among other films that pushed the Production Code to its limits were *Jewel Robbery* (1932), in which a jewel thief (William Powell) hands out marijuana cigarettes to subdue his victims; *Baby Face* (1933), with Barbara Stanwyck sleeping her way to the top of the social ladder; *Tarzan and His Mate* (1934), in which the title characters (Johnny Weissmuller and Maureen O'Sullivan) are often less than fully clothed (including an underwater nude swim scene that was cut from the picture for several decades); *Gold Diggers of 1933*, for its display of scantily clad female dancers; Cecil B. DeMille's all-star epics *The Sign of the Cross* (1932) and *Cleopatra* (1934), for various glimpses of nudity (which were deleted for re-releases throughout the Production Code era); and many, many more, including several films each featuring Jean Harlow's flimsy, barely-there clothing and Mae West's bawdy double-entendres.

Even the queen of animated shorts, Betty Boop, was chided for her scandalously skimpy outfits. If you compare her cartoons during those first four years with 'toons released later in the decade, the adjustment in her post-mid-'30s clothing is obvious.

By 1934, there was hanging over the industry a serious threat of boycotts of movies found to be immoral. One powerful lobbying group in particular sent studio chiefs into a panic. That year the Catholic Church established the National Legion of Decency—which at the time also included Protestant and Jewish members—to evaluate

Fay Wray in the pre-Code King Kong *(1933) —RKO*

motion picture content and urge the faithful to stay away from offensive films. The Legion of Decency demonstrated that it carried a big stick, and almost single-handedly prompted the member studios of the MPPDA to, reluctantly, allow Hays' Production Code to begin enforcing a seal of approval. If a studio film was to be released to American theaters, it had to carry the seal, and to carry the seal it had to closely adhere to the Code's rules.

In June 1934, the SRC was officially retitled the Production Code Administration and Hays hired censor Joseph Breen to head it up and be his main enforcer. With a remarkable amount of power suddenly at his disposal, Hays became a dogmatic dictator of the rules, so much so that the Production Code came to be referred to more often as "The Hays Code." Breen was his pit bull and they made for an unpopular duo among Hollywood's corps of writers and directors.

For the next twenty-five years or so, Hollywood studio films—those made from 1934 into the late 1950s—cleaned up their act, and filmmakers learned how to imply and suggest rather than graphically display. Did Rick and Ilsa (Humphrey Bogart and Ingrid Bergman) go to bed together after rekindling their love in *Casablanca* (1942)? Probably, but it had to be hinted at rather than shown (not that the film suffers in the least).

From time to time during the late 1930s and through the '40s there were battles over certain films, but for more than two decades the studios and filmmakers generally caved to the demands of the Code, with only the occasional compromise. As a result, filmmakers would find creative ways to get around the Code, making powerful films in the process. Three prime examples as the 1940s wound down were *Notorious* (1946), *Johnny Belinda* (1948), and *Pinky* (1949).

A famous scene in *Notorious* has Ingrid Bergman and Cary Grant in a clinch lasting more than two minutes. Watching the film today, even 21st century viewers can't help but be moved by how remarkably sensuous it is to see these characters' unbridled passions at play, and it's still easy to come away thinking of it as one very lengthy kiss. But as prolonged kisses were forbidden, that would violate the Code's so-called "three-second rule," which allowed that a smooch could last no longer than three seconds.

So director Alfred Hitchcock shot Bergman and Grant in close-up, instructing them to embrace, kiss for a couple of seconds, then put a head on a shoulder or nibble an ear, then kiss again for a few seconds, then they would be interrupted by the telephone, and while answering kiss again . . . and so it goes, for some two-and-a-half minutes. Since no single kiss between them lasted for more than three seconds, the Production Code censors could not object.

The studio (RKO) took advantage of this by using the moment in its promotional materials, with posters showing the faces of Bergman and Grant as they nuzzle. (For modern moviemakers, this sequence is instructive, demonstrating that it's actually more effective to portray gentle, loving, romantic foreplay as opposed to the kind of graphic and crude jump-into-bed sex scenes we so often see in movies today.)

Johnny Belinda was the first film to treat the subject of rape in a realistic manner. Up to this point, the topic, when it was allowed to arise at all, was handled in a manner so oblique that moviegoers sometimes weren't quite sure if a rape had occurred.

But *Johnny Belinda* is straightforward in its story of a gentle deaf mute named Belinda (Jane Wyman in an Oscar-winning performance), who, after enduring the horror of being raped by a thuggish neighbor, finds she is pregnant. This leads to a firestorm of gossip and lies in her small backward village, some of it aimed at an innocent doctor (Lew Ayres) who has been teaching Belinda to sign, and thus communicate with others for the first time. (Again, there is nothing graphic, but in this artful presentation there is also no question about what happens.)

Pinky also brought forth a formerly taboo subject in a manner that was engaging, powerful, and unashamed, impossible for moviegoers to ignore, with its story of miscegenation. Jeanne Crain has the title role as a young woman who must come to terms with her mixed heritage in the racist South after she has been away to a northern school, where she has been studying nursing while passing as white. She has also fallen in love with a white doctor and plans to return and marry him.

But fate and the wisdom of her grandmother (Ethel Waters) and a local doctor (Kenny Washington) conspire to force Pinky into the realization that she can never be happy or fulfilled if she's living a lie. The film still has some punch today, although it suffers from one concession the studio (Twentieth Century Fox) was unwilling to make—it would not cast a light-skinned black actress for the role (say, Dorothy Dandridge or Lena Horne, both active in Hollywood at the time), instead giving the role to Crain, a white actress. Although, it must be added that Crain is very good and earned her only Academy Award nomination for the role.

By the early 1950s, however, post-World War II audiences were craving more realistic stories over the eternal happy endings provided by Hollywood, and this resulted in some serious grumbling in the ranks. Hints that there could be a breakdown of the Production Code's effectiveness turned into a real threat, thanks in part to the retirement in 1945 of the Code's despot, Will H. Hays, followed by the retirement nine years later of his taskmaster, Joseph Breen. The popularity of foreign films—particularly those that had begun arriving steadily from France, Italy, and Sweden—also played a part.

European filmmakers were becoming bolder, especially in terms of how they depicted sexuality, and their films could be shown in American theaters without being bound by the Production Code. No seal of approval was necessary since the distributors didn't belong to the U.S. studios' trade association, which by now was calling itself the Motion Picture Association of America (MPAA).

That boldness began to have an influence on American writers and directors who felt that if filmmakers outside the United States could get away with more specific, and sometimes, more graphic material shown on American theater screens, it was a signal that the times were indeed a'changing, and they should also have the freedom to create adult films with adult themes.

In addition, as television became popular in the early 1950s, the motion picture industry was beginning to feel threatened by the fact that filmgoers could stay home and watch movies for free, instead of heading out to local theaters where they had to pay. In order to compete, more and more theatrical films were being made in color instead of black and white; widescreen processes, starting with CinemaScope, were quickly becoming the standard; and such gimmicks as 3D were also being employed as an incentive to get people into theater seats. And since TV was compelled to be family-friendly, the thinking was that movies should not be afraid to be more pronounced in their maturity as a way of luring an audience away from the "idiot box."

One of the first to successfully crack the barrier of the Production Code's seal of approval was director Otto Preminger, whose popular Hollywood productions during the 1940s included the Joan Crawford romance *Daisy Kenyon* (1947), with Henry Fonda and Dana Andrews; the costume soap opera *Forever Amber* (1947), starring Linda Darnell and adapted from a much racier novel; and especially the film noir classic *Laura* (1944), with Dana Andrews, Clifton Webb, Vincent Price, and which provided a real showcase role for Gene Tierney.

Under the Production Code, Preminger's edgier material for these and other films had always been clipped in the script stage, but in 1953 he challenged the Code as he prepared to film a stage play called *The Moon Is Blue*, which treated the subject of seduction in a lighthearted manner, and which featured characters engaging in discussions of a sexual nature, using such heretofore banished words as "virgin," "seduce," and "mistress."

Although by today's standards the banter between Maggie McNamara, William Holden, and David Niven in *The Moon Is Blue* is coy and innocent, even quaint, to the Production Code censors of 1953, the script was unacceptable. But for the first time, the studio (United Artists) backed Preminger and he shot the film his way, without any changes in the screenplay. And, of course, the finished product was denied the Code's seal of approval.

As you might expect, the publicity this generated only made the picture all the more alluring to moviegoers, and it was released to a few theaters that were willing to buck the system and present it as an "adults-only" presentation, a sort of experiment to see if it would make any money. It did, and based on that success, most (but not all) theaters around the country agreed to accept it for regular engagements. (There is an episode of the *M*A*S*H* television series that has Hawkeye and B.J., played by Alan Alda and Mike Farrell, trying to get a copy of *The Moon Is Blue* to show in the camp.)

The success of *The Moon Is Blue* put a major dent in the Production Code's power, and two subsequent Preminger pictures didn't help. Emboldened by the success of *The Moon Is Blue*, among Preminger's next few films were two that even more aggressively pushed against boundaries previously considered sacrosanct: *The Man With The Golden Arm* (1955), starring Frank Sinatra as a drug addict, was also released without the Code's seal of approval, and the 1959 courtroom drama *Anatomy of a Murder*, starring James Stewart and George C.

James Stewart and Lee Remick in Otto Preminger's Anatomy of a Murder *(1959) —Columbia*

Scott as lawyers on opposite sides of a murder trial, contains frank, clinical dialogue about sexuality and rape.

By now, other filmmakers were also challenging the Production Code's authority, and, as the 1960s kicked in, the walls were beginning to crumble. Controversial movies that would never have been made just a few years earlier were starting to come out of the Hollywood studios on a regular basis. In the late 1950s, such then daring pictures as *Baby Doll, Suddenly Last Summer, Pillow Talk,* and *Some Like it Hot* were introducing sexuality in a way that American movie audiences were unaccustomed to, but which they, nonetheless, embraced.

And the early 1960s brought, among others, such groundbreakers as *Psycho* (in terms of the violence it portrayed); *BUtterfield 8*, *The Apartment*, *The Chapman Report,* and *Lolita* (with adult attitudes toward sex); *The Pawnbroker* (with female nudity); and the first three James Bond movies, *Dr. No*, *From Russia With Love*, and *Goldfinger* (with violence punctuated by humor and unbridled promiscuity). As the '60s wound down, Hollywood films became even more graphic, led by *Who's Afraid of Virginia Woolf* (expanding the level of foul language); *Alfie*, *The Graduate,* and *Midnight Cowboy* (pushing sexual standards); and *Bonnie and Clyde* and *The Wild Bunch* (extended, graphic scenes of bloody violence).

By 1966, the federal government was on the receiving end of no small amount of pressure to do something about motion picture content, and in turn the government was beginning to put pressure on the movie studios. That year the Motion Picture Association of America reached out to Jack Valenti, a Washington press advisor and lobbyist, urging him to leave politics for Hollywood and help resolve the situation. Valenti became president of the MPAA, and he immediately began sowing the seeds that would, as he would later put it, help the movie industry "grow up" and still stave off the intervention of federal censorship.

During his first year in office, one of Valenti's initial moves was to revise the Production Code's seal of approval to include a parental warning: the letters "SMA" for posters and other advertising materials, indicating "Suggested for Mature Audiences." But that was intended as merely a temporary measure while Valenti began work in earnest on what would become the Classification and Rating Administration (CARA), under the auspices of the MPAA. Two years later the rating board was in place and the first ratings were stamped on films in late 1968.

Initially, the ratings were:

G (General Audience): All ages admitted, nothing offensive.

M (Mature Audience): Some material not suitable for children, parents should offer guidance.

R (Restricted): No one under 16 admitted without a parent or adult guardian.

X: No one under 18 admitted (with or without an adult).

Some changes followed rather quickly in those first few months and years as the rating system got off to a wobbly start:

The age for R-rated films was quickly bumped up to seventeen.

In January 1970 the M was changed to GP, and then, in 1972 it became the PG that is still in use today.

In 1984, the PG-13 was created as a stopgap between PG and R.

The X, which was the only rating not trademarked by the MPAA, was more or less co-opted by the pornographic film industry, and, therefore went virtually unused for most of its existence (with some notorious early exceptions, such as *Midnight Cowboy* in 1969 and *Last Tango in Paris* in 1972). Ultimately the X was phased out and replaced in 1990 by NC-17.

Here are the ratings today, as defined by CARA on its website, www.filmratings.com:

G (General Audience): The motion picture contains nothing that would offend parents for viewing by their children.

PG (Parental Guidance Suggested): Parents are urged to use 'parental guidance,' as the motion picture may contain some material parents might not like their younger children to view.

PG-13 (Parents Strongly Cautioned): Parents are urged to be cautious. Some material may be inappropriate for pre-teenagers.

R (Restricted): Contains some adult material. Parents are urged to learn more about the motion picture before taking their younger children with them. Generally, it is

Jon Voight and Dustin Hoffman in John Schlesinger's Midnight Cowboy *(1969) —United Artists*

not appropriate for parents to bring their young children with them to R-rated motion pictures.

NC-17: Patently adult. Children are not admitted.

The CARA website also offers these expanded explanations of what is considered for each rating by those who sit on the board and make the decisions:

A G-rated motion picture contains nothing in theme, language, nudity, sex, violence, or other matters that, in the view of the Rating Board, would offend parents whose younger children view the motion picture. The G rating is not a 'certificate of approval,' nor does it signify a 'children's' motion picture. Some snippets of language may go beyond polite conversation, but they are common everyday expressions. No stronger words are present in G-rated motion pictures. Depictions of violence are minimal. No nudity, sex scenes, or drug use are present in the motion picture.

A PG-rated motion picture should be investigated by parents before they let their younger children attend. The PG rating indicates, in the view of the Rating Board, that parents may consider some material unsuitable for their children, and parents should make that decision. The more mature themes in some PG-rated motion pictures may call for parental guidance. There may be some profanity and some depictions of violence or brief nudity. But these elements are not deemed so intense as to require that parents be strongly cautioned beyond the suggestion of parental guidance. There is no drug use content in a PG-rated motion picture.

A PG-13 rating is a sterner warning by the Rating Board to parents to determine whether their children under age thirteen should view the motion picture, as some material might not be suited for them. A PG-13 motion picture may go beyond the PG rating in theme, violence, nudity, sensuality, language, adult activities, or other elements, but does not reach the restricted R category. The theme of the motion picture by itself will not result in a rating greater than PG-13, although depictions of activities related to a mature theme may result in a restricted rating for the motion picture. Any drug use will initially require at least a PG-13 rating. More than brief nudity will require at least a PG-13 rating, but such nudity in a PG-13 rated motion picture generally will not be sexually oriented. There may be depictions of violence in a PG-13 movie, but generally not realistic and extreme or persistent violence. A motion picture's single use of one of the harsher sexually-derived words, though only as an expletive, initially requires at least a PG-13 rating. More than one such expletive requires an R rating, as must even one of those words used in a sexual context. The Rating Board, nevertheless, may rate such a motion picture PG-13 if, based on a special vote by a two-thirds majority, the Raters feel that most American parents would believe that a PG-13 rating is appropriate because of the context or manner in which the words are used or because the use of those words in the motion picture is inconspicuous.

An R-rated motion picture, in the view of the Rating Board, contains some adult material. An R-rated motion picture may include adult themes, adult activity, hard language, intense or persistent violence, sexually-oriented nudity, drug abuse, or other elements, so that parents are counseled to take this rating very seriously. Children under seventeen are not allowed to attend R-rated motion pictures unaccompanied by a parent or adult guardian. Parents are strongly urged to find out more about R-rated motion pictures in determining their suitability for their children. Generally, it is not appropriate for parents to bring their young children with them to R-rated motion pictures.

An NC-17 rated motion picture is one that, in the view of the Rating Board, most parents would consider patently too adult for their children. No children will be admitted. NC-17 does not mean 'obscene' or 'pornographic' and should not be construed as a negative judgment in any sense. The rating simply signals that the content is appropriate only for an adult audience. An NC-17 rating can be based on violence, sex, aberrational behavior, drug abuse, or any other element that most parents would consider too strong, and, therefore, off-limits for viewing by their children.

These ratings are used for feature films released in theaters and on home video. Television programs and video games have their own rating systems and are completely separate from those administered by CARA.

Chapter 2

THE MPAA AND CARA

Respond to Criticism

For two decades, from 1974 to 1994, Richard D. Heffner was the chairman of the Classification and Rating Administration. He was the guy that worked day to day with the members of the rating board, and, when necessary, would cast a deciding vote. But the public face of the ratings was very much Jack Valenti.

During my years as a movie critic, I had occasion to interview Valenti several times for both the *Deseret News* and KSL, and he was always gracious and chatty and ready for anything. Valenti served as President of the Motion Picture Association of America for thirty-eight years, during which time he earned a reputation for being irascible and feisty, especially when it came to standing up for CARA. He retired in 2004 at age eighty-two and died three years later. (The current president of the MPAA is former Connecticut Senator Christopher J. Dodd.)

Though Valenti has been gone for a few years now, the creator, chief instigator, and omnipresent cheerleader of the movie-rating system still seems to hover over the board. The ratings remain today largely what he created more than four decades ago, and, for good or ill, the party line at the board hasn't changed much.

The current head of CARA, Joan Graves, has this statement posted on the CARA website (www.filmratings.com):

> The ratings system exists for one purpose: to inform parents about the content of films. Our ratings reflect how we believe a majority of American parents, not just from large cities on the coasts, but everywhere in between, would rate a film. It's a responsibility we take very seriously.
>
> When we assign ratings to films, we do not make qualitative judgments; we are not film critics or censors. We are parents who ask ourselves the same important question during every screening: What would I want to know about this film before I allow my child to see it? The board makes ratings decisions based on the film in its entirety, not by comparison to other films.
>
> Decisions are guided by established criteria for each rating category, which includes a few rules that trigger an automatic rating. For instance, any depiction of drug use results in at least a PG-13.
>
> The restrictive ratings, R and NC-17, are not a judgment or punishment. The ratings simply convey to parents that, in the case of an R, a film has elements strong enough that parents should learn more about them before taking their children. In the case of an NC-17, the rating is unequivocal. The movie is patently adult. We are not saying adults can't and shouldn't see these films.
>
> There's a sentiment in our industry that a film judged as 'good,' 'worthwhile,' or 'acclaimed' by critics and audiences should be given a less restrictive rating so more people—namely children—can see it. But it's important to note that rarely, if ever, do we hear from parents that a film given an R or NC-17 should get a lower rating so it's more accessible to their children.

Graves extrapolated on this a bit in a recent interview with Carey Bryson for About.com (kidstvmovies.about.com), after introducing Graves as the head of CARA and the only member whose identity is made public, and as the one responsible for choosing the other board members.

Bryson asked how Graves keeps her "finger on the pulse of American parents all across the United States," to which Graves replied: "We do run surveys from time to time and focus groups in areas across the country. We ask objectively how parents feel about certain things, including language, so we know we're not just hearing from complainers. I do hear from a lot of parents via email and on the phone, sometimes letters. And what I want to do is make sure that I'm getting the right information, not just hearing from the people who are overly conservative."

Graves was also asked to respond to a statement by documentary filmmaker Michael Moore, who criticized the board for its rating of *Bully*, a documentary by Lee Hirsch. *Bully* went through some public controversy when it received an R rating for the use of the f-word several times, but was cited by critics and those inside the industry as a film kids needed to see. Ultimately, Hirsch agreed to bleep a few (but not all) usages of the word and the film received a PG-13 on appeal. Moore said of the rating board's attitude toward language, "Their strict guidelines are outdated and rigid, and I don't understand why they don't see that."

Graves said :

> I think it's easy for an adult in the media to think that harsh language doesn't matter to parents. And it may not matter to parents once their kids are thirty, and forty, and maybe in their twenties (laughs), but we know from really direct questions in our surveys that they do care. They want to be the arbiter of what their kids are exposed to. So, what they want us to do is give them the information and then they'll act on it.
>
> . . . I'm a mother of two girls, and I know that my girls were very different and still are. One was more fearful than

> the other. The older one was more fearful, actually, and I would choose movies differently for each one of them, and I think that's one of the things that our system allows parents to do . . . to take into consideration each child's sensibilities and make decisions according to what they know.

Bryson also asked how many movies Graves actually watches. "It depends on how strong they are," Graves said. "Sometimes filmmakers who are submitting a film know they're going to have a problem . . . and they call and say, 'We may have trouble with this, would you make sure you see it so we can talk to you?' In which case, I will. I read synopses of films, and anything that looks especially violent or

Alex in Lee Hirsch's documentary Bully *(2012) —The Weinstein Company*

horror-like or troublesome, I make sure I see. I'll put it this way: I see a lot of films I wouldn't choose to see in real life (laughs)."

In subsequent chapters there are examples of many movies that have been rated G, PG, PG-13 and R, spanning the decades since the ratings' inception through 2012, and you can judge for yourself whether the rating system seems to be working. See if you, as a parent, would indeed agree with the ratings given to various films by this board of "parents."

It is, perhaps, instructive to see the intent behind the ratings as driven by Valenti himself, how it works, and what it means, especially since his template is obviously still in place.

These are comments gleaned from several interviews I did with Valenti over the years for the *Deseret News* and KSL, in which he explained what CARA tries to do and for whom the ratings chiefly exist. Valenti emphasized often that, despite a common misconception among some moviegoers, the ratings are not laws and cannot be legally enforced.

"The rating system is a voluntary system whereby producers submit their films to the rating board in California, and then the rating board gives a rating," Valenti said. "The whole objective of the rating system is to give parents some advance cautionary warning, so that the parent can make the decision as to what movies his or her child should or should not see."

Valenti would bristle at the word "censorship," explaining that, unlike the Production Code of the 1930s and '40s, CARA requires nothing of filmmakers, but rather merely reacts to the movies they make. "This is all a voluntary system today. That is, no producer is forced to cut one millimeter of his film, if he—the producer or the director—doesn't choose to. So, it isn't censorship at all. And if any editing is done, it's because that is the choice of the director or the producer."

Enforcement of the ratings, he explained, particularly the R rating, is entirely up to various movie theaters around the country. "The National Association of Theater Owners, which is a partner in this enterprise, tells me that some 75-80 percent of the theaters are enforcing the ratings. If a parent finds out they aren't, I suggest that they use a good old American tradition of going down to the theater owner and saying, 'Look, a lot of families live around this theater. We want you to enforce these ratings.' And I think most parents will get some kind of a favorable response."

The structure of the rating board is much the same today as it was when Valenti talked about it in the mid-1990s. The CARA website (www.filmratings.com) states that "The rating system exists to give parents clear, concise information about a film's content, in order to

Colin Firth and Geoffrey Rush in The King's Speech *(2010) —The Weinstein Company*

help them determine whether a movie is suitable for their children," although whether that is what happens is up for debate. And the site adds, "Ratings are assigned by a board of parents. Their job is to reflect what they believe would be the majority view of their fellow American parents in assigning a rating to a film."

Valenti described the members as "men and women, blacks, whites, Hispanics, Protestant, Jewish, Catholic. We try . . . to get a microcosm of the country. And they stay on the board two, three years at a time, and then they leave and new people come on. We try to make sure there's a replenishment of new people. The sole criterion is that you must be a parent—(each) rating board member has to be a parent. Other than that, we want them to love movies, to be intelligent, to care about the ratings themselves."

"Board members are hired as they would be in any business," Valenti said. "They write in and say they'd like to become a member of the board. Sometimes a teacher will take a sabbatical and want to stay on the board a year or two. Letters come in from all over the country, we interview them and we pick them. There's nothing mysterious about it."

And it's a full-time job with the identities of the board members withheld. "And the reason is," Valenti said, "I don't want some angry producer, mad because he got a more severe rating than he thought he deserved, harassing these people, either by letter or phone call. It is a full-time job and they're paid to do this. They see two, three pictures a day. So, if you don't like movies, you won't like this job."

As for how they rate the films, "Sex, violence, theme, general demeanor of the film are all subjectively valued by this board. It's very difficult to have precise rules. What is too much violence, for example? That's a subjective enterprise."

The only real hard-and-fast rules the rating board must abide by really aren't all that hard and fast. A recent rule is that any form of drug abuse automatically gets a PG-13, and may help push a movie toward an R, depending on the context. Smoking has also become a factor in deciding a rating, though there is no specific rule attached to it.

But there is one rule that seems to concern people the most—true then and true now: The language rule that has to do with the so-called "f-word," which may be spoken only once in a non-sexual context to earn a PG-13. If the word is spoken two or more times, or if it is spoken even once in a sexual context, the film will be rated R.

The verbiage on CARA's website is this:

> A motion picture's single use of one of the harsher sexually-derived words, though only as an expletive, initially requires at least a PG-13 rating. More than one such expletive requires an R rating, as must even one of these words used in a sexual context. The Rating Board, nevertheless, may rate such a motion picture PG-13 if, based on a special vote by a two-thirds majority, the Raters feel that most American parents would believe that a PG-13 rating is appropriate because of the context or manner in which the words are used or because the use of those words in a motion picture is inconspicuous.

In other words, it's a definite maybe.

According to Valenti. "The Rating Board has the power in this automatic rule—that if they believe the film is otherwise fairly benign, and that the language is not part of an overall hard realism—they have the power to say, 'OK, we'll forgive that and give it a PG-13.' But it depends on what the rest of the film is like."

And that is becoming more and more obvious today. In late 2011, the Los Angeles Times decried a sort of "f-word creep," as that expletive was showing up two, three, or four times in certain PG-13 movies, but according to Valenti back in the mid-1990s, that's always been the case.

When the documentary *Bully* received an R in early 2012, the rating was challenged by the film's distributor, which wanted a PG-13 so kids could see a film on an important subject that related to high schoolers. Eventually, the filmmakers bleeped out three of its original six f-words and got the PG-13.

Back when I challenged Valenti on the R rating, which seemed at the time—and still seems today—to be rather inconsistent, he didn't disagree. At the time I used the disparate examples of *A Few Good Men* and *Basic Instinct*, two films that really don't belong in the same rating pool. Today's examples might be that such soft-R films as *The King's Speech* or *The Descendants* hardly belong in the same arena as *The Girl with the Dragon Tattoo* and *The Cabin in the Woods.*

Valenti explained:

> [It's] because you can't draw fine lines in this thing and have the R split up into four or five different sections. What R says is, 'There is adult material in this film, Mr. and Mrs. Parent.

Kristen Connolly in* Cabin in the Woods *(2011) —Lionsgate

> Therefore, we caution you, we really strongly caution you, to find out more about this film either by seeing it yourself or reading the reviews or reading in magazines or talking to a neighbor who has seen the film. Check it out before you allow your young children to see it.' And that runs the whole gamut of R films. While there might be hard, harder, and hardest in an R film, all of them contain adult material, as far as the rating board view is concerned.

I also asked why it seems that PG and PG-13 movies often have content that is inappropriate for children. He replied:

> I have not agreed with all the ratings of the rating board. I have to say that honestly to you. But keep in mind that the rating board is composed of people like you and me—they're human beings . . . So the fact is that maybe we do make some mistakes from time to time, but they try to do the best that they can, and all parents are different. There are 250 million people in this country, and some of them are upset by violence, some are upset by sex, some by language, some by theme. So, it is impossible to please everybody all the time. I think disappointment and error are built into any kind of man-made operation like this.

As to whether the board has gone soft over the years, Valenti said:

> Let me ask a counter-question? Has the society changed? I think the answer is, it has changed greatly. I know that as an observer, there seems to be much more violence in our society, people getting killed more. There is a lessening of some of the old values. There's been insurrection on the streets and rebellion on the campuses and the rise of feminism, which has changed the way we look at things—and I think for the better. And there have been all the civil rights laws that have come in, that have changed the kind of way we look at oth-

ers of different race and nationalities. There has been a lot of change in the mores and the customs of the society that have reflected itself in a rougher, sometimes, kind of society.

So, it's impossible that movies, the most creative of all the art forms, would be immune to these changes in the social landscape. So, the answer to your question is, 'Sure.' I think what might have been an R in 1966 or '68 today probably is a PG-13. Keep in mind that an X-rated picture—which was the adult category up until [the NC-17 replaced it]—an X-rated picture, *Midnight Cowboy*, won the Academy Award [for best picture]. Since then, the mores and customs have changed and there've been no 'adult' (NC-17) pictures that have been nominated for an Academy Award, much less won it.

It should be noted that the number of movies rated each year ranges from 800 to 900, according to the CARA website. Most people won't see that many in a lifetime. Compare that to the roughly 250 titles that come through Salt Lake City theaters each year—and Salt Lake City is considered a real moviegoing town—and then factor in myriad straight-to-DVD movies, and the number of movies submitted to CARA seems overwhelming.

Most of these movies will never be made available to the general public, which means that the people on the rating board sit through an awful lot of movies that were later deemed not good enough to be distributed, the vast majority from independent filmmakers. Considering what does get distributed, it's mind-boggling to imagine how low quality those other films must be.

Also, the distributors pay a percentage of each film's budget to have it rated, which can get pretty pricey for big-budget blockbusters. And advertising materials that carry ratings must also be approved by CARA.

The majority of films that pass through the board receive R ratings, and that's been pretty stable since CARA's inception.

Valenti said:

Yes, the majority of the films are rated R. One of the things that I should point out is ratings have absolutely nothing to do with box office. I have what I call 'Valenti's Law,' and that is, 'If you make a film that a lot of people want to see, no rating will hurt you. If you make a film that few people want to see, no rating will help you.'

How many people do you know, families, men and women, who wake up in the morning and say, 'Tonight, let's go see an R-rated movie,' or, 'Let's go see a PG-13.' They don't do that. They say, 'What's playing? Oh, I want to see Clint Eastwood's new film,' or, 'I want to see (a specific title).' They don't go to movies based on ratings, for goodness sake.

Chapter 3

ARE R RATINGS ALWAYS DESERVED?

R-rated films can be as hard as what critics call "torture-porn," such as the extremely graphic, gory, bloody horror movies of the *Saw* and *Hostel* series (as well as any number of modern gangster and zombie movies), or they can be as soft as, well, some examples that may surprise you.

As you can see from the explanations of the ratings, what it really comes down to are the whims of a panel of board members who may not even agree with each other. Though CARA won't release any specific voting examples, it's possible that the panel could be fairly divided between members who are younger and older, who have more liberal leanings sitting with those who are more conservative, people whose votes might be split evenly between a PG and an R for a particular film, or between R and NC-17, in which case they rely upon CARA's chairperson, currently Joan Graves, to cast the deciding vote. Graves has been affiliated with CARA since 1988 and was appointed as its head by Jack Valenti in 2000, and she is the one who has the final say.

So, it's safe to suggest that simply dismissing all R-rated movies as something to be avoided is too sweeping a statement, too much of a generality. Even the most conservative audience members probably do not regret having seen *The Killing Fields* (1984) or *A Few Good Men* (1992) or *Schindler's List* (1993) or *Saving Private Ryan* (1998) or *The King's Speech* (2010), and most would describe these films as perhaps deserving the R rating, but also having qualities that make them special movies worth experiencing. On the other hand, others might feel that the amount of violence or profanity is too much, regardless of the film's quality, and they aren't sorry they skipped seeing them. And I don't think anyone is going to suggest they are movies for children.

On the other hand, there are some films that receive R ratings that just seem to come out of left field. Take *Psycho,* for example. No, not Gus Van Sant's 1998 remake, which earned its R by making the violence more bloody and including some unnecessary sexual material, nor the 1983 and 1986 sequels by Anthony Perkins, which also earned R ratings with the usual violent and sexual exploitation elements.

Would you believe that the original black-and-white Alfred Hitchcock classic is also rated R? That's right, although, as you probably realize, it wasn't always rated R.

In 1960 when *Psycho* was initially released, there were no ratings yet. Then, in 1968 when Universal Pictures was about to give the film a theatrical re-release in the first months of the ratings' existence, *Psycho* was submitted to the board and came away with an M, the equivalent at the time of what is now PG.

But in the fall of 1984, when it came time to prep *Psycho* for its first home-video release (on VHS tape), Universal felt the out-of-date M rating, which had not been used for some fifteen years, would be confusing to the public, particularly the young movie-renting demographic that was (and is) specifically courted by the film industry. The studio probably felt confident that *Psycho* would get a PG, but to the surprise of Universal executives, Hitchcock fans, and the industry at large, *Psycho* received an R. Say what?

Considering the amount of violence in some PG-rated movies released around the same time, in early 1984 when the PG-13 was still a few months away, and given the relatively oblique and bloodless violence depicted in *Psycho*, giving Hitchcock's classic an R rating seemed ludicrous. At the time I cited the then current PG-rated *Conan the Destroyer*, *Romancing the Stone,* and *Cloak & Dagger* as examples of films that displayed more gore than Hitchcock's *Psycho*—and all three, of course, retain their PG ratings today.

On the R-rated end of the spectrum, in the 1980s such franchise series as *Halloween*, *Friday the 13th,* and *A Nightmare on Elm Street* were churning out gore-filled sequels, each competing to incrementally up the ante on shock value, and not just with violence but also with sex and nudity. And when you think about how much further gory horror films have gone in the 21st century, having *Psycho* on DVD with an R rating now seems all the more preposterous.

But unless a movie's rating is appealed or it is later submitted to CARA to be re-rated for some reason, it is what it is. From time to time old movies from the late 1960s and early '70s still show up on DVD with "M" or "GP" ratings, since they've never been re-submitted to the board (the 2012 Blu-ray upgrade of the 1972 Robert Redford film *Jeremiah Johnson* is an example, as the back of the box clearly displays a GP rating). For some reason Universal has chosen not to appeal the R on *Psycho*, perhaps believing that an R rating might be a good thing, that young people will see an R-rated *Psycho* in a rental store and be more inclined to pick it up. After all, how scary would a black-and-white PG or PG-13 horror movie be?

Hitchcock worked for most of the major motion-picture companies during his Hollywood tenure, and the rights to his films are owned by no less than eight studios, with the bulk of his later classics under the Universal Pictures banner. Universal financed and produced *Shadow of a Doubt*, *Saboteur*, *The Birds*, *Marnie*, *Torn Curtain*, *Topaz*, *Frenzy*, and *Family Plot*. And the Universal catalog also includes six of Hitchcock's Paramount Pictures productions that were purchased by Universal somewhere along the way: *Rope*, *Rear Window*, *The Trouble With Harry*, *The Man Who Knew Too Much*, *Vertigo*, and *Psycho*.

Hitchcock only made three movies after the ratings came into being: *Topaz*, which received an M in 1969; *Frenzy*, which earned an R in 1972; and *Family Plot*, rated PG in 1976. Note that *Frenzy*, in which Hitchcock used graphic violence, nudity, and foul language for the first time in the story of a vicious rapist/killer on the loose in contemporary London, is the only film he made that earned its R rating the first time around.

All of the other titles in the Universal-Hitchcock catalog have been re-rated to PG, save *The Birds*, which carries a PG-13, and possibly *Topaz*. For some reason, according to the CARA website, *Topaz* does not appear to have been formally re-rated from its original M rating, yet there is nonetheless, an official PG rating tag on the print itself (after the end credits), as well as "PG" being printed on some home-video boxes. Curiously, in the *Alfred Hitchcock: The Masterpiece*

The famous scene of crows gathering on a jungle gym in Alfred Hitchcock's The Birds *(1963) —Universal*

Collection DVD set, printed on the *Topaz* disc is the phrase "not rated," even though that PG tag is on the print, and vintage poster art on the box cover clearly reveals the original M.

No wonder movie ratings can seem confusing.

Another bizarre rating example is a trio of made-for-television *Gunsmoke* movies, belated sequels to the legendary TV series that starred James Arness and ran an amazing twenty years on CBS, from 1955-75. The trio of movies was released on DVD in 2004—both as individual discs and in a three-pack—by Paramount Home Entertainment/CBS: *Gunsmoke: Return to Dodge* (1987), *Gunsmoke: The Last Apache* (1990), and *Gunsmoke: To the Last Man* (1992). In 2003, just prior to their home-video release the next year, each was rated by CARA, and while one received a PG-13, two were rated R! The explanation for the ratings on all three is "violence."

These DVDs were made from prints of the films exactly as they were shown on CBS during prime time in the late 1980s and early '90s. That is to say, they were not edited to change any footage, nothing was added that would make them any more violent than when they were originally shown on commercial television more than two decades before. And at that time there was no special audience or parental warning preceding these shows to alert parents that they were particularly violent. Today, there are often such warnings on the *CSI* and *Law & Order* franchises, as well as many other prime-time network programs, that think nothing of graphic violence and gore far beyond what these films contain.

Understand that I'm not arguing that these *Gunsmoke* films aren't violent; they are. There's plenty of gunplay, with bullets hitting and killing people. But the R ratings put two of these *Gunsmoke* movies in the same category as *The Cabin in the Woods* and *The Raven*, to use a pair of 2012 examples of movies that splatter blood and gore in the extreme, as well as all the R-rated horror movies that are available on DVD. It also suggests that the *Gunsmoke* films are more violent than such 2012 PG-13 fare as *The Avengers*, *Battleship*, *The Bourne Legacy*, and *Skyfall*—which is simply not the case.

There are many less famous examples, films you may or may not recognize that also point up discrepancies in the R rating category.

In September 1983—before the PG-13 rating was created—I reviewed a little horror movie called *Nightmares* that was released with an R rating. I didn't think much of it going in, but after watching it I wondered why in the world it was rated R, since it seemed fairly innocuous. So I did a little research and discovered that the film had initially received a PG rating but the studio, Universal Pictures, resubmitted it to the board and came away with an R. Quite often movies that receive R ratings will go back to the board for an appeal and come away with a PG, but going from a PG to an R was new to my experience. So, naturally, my curiosity was aroused.

At the time the popular thinking was that an R-rated horror movie makes more money than a PG-rated horror movie (although that didn't account for the popularity of *Poltergeist* and *Twilight Zone—The Movie*, two Steven Spielberg-produced pictures that did well during this period). So, those straight-thinking movie moguls at Universal apparently decided that *Nightmares*, an anthology film with four stand-alone horror stories, had better carry an R or gore fans would think it didn't deliver. And actually, in terms of R-level excess, it didn't.

Nightmares has no profanity, no nudity, no sex, and no gore, save a bit of blood in the opening sequence where a police officer is attacked and killed by a stereotypical movie "slasher," a mental institution escapee. There is dripping blood and a bloody corpse, and at the end of that segment the killer is shot dead. But the way it was depicted wasn't even close to R-rated horror of the period, and in fact, wasn't as bad as many PG-rated thrillers of the period.

Then I spoke to a friend who had seen a closed exhibitor's screening of *Nightmares* some months before its release, and he said there was no police officer sequence in the print he saw. Further research revealed that *Nightmares* was a made-for-TV film that the studio inexplicably felt was strong enough to release theatrically. So the question became, did Universal shoot that opening sequence for the express purpose of getting an R rating?

Maybe someone ought to explain to these wizards of marketing that all they really had to do was add a particular profanity to the soundtrack—the word that is automatically supposed to require an R rating if it's used more than once. True, that would have been equally deceitful to the gore-loving horror hounds they were wooing, but it could have saved them some added production dollars on a picture that was never going to recoup its cost.

In 1991, two films—*Guilty by Suspicion* and *Class Action*—opened across the country on the same day, offering a vivid illustration of how arbitrary the ratings can seem. I gave each a positive review and referred to them as "excellent adult dramas of the kind we get all too rarely these days."

Guilty by Suspicion is an examination of the House Un-American Activities Committee witch-hunt in the 1950s, with Robert De Niro as a movie director who finds himself on the Hollywood blacklist. *Class Action* is a father-daughter reconciliation drama set against a courtroom battle, starring Gene Hackman and Mary Elizabeth Mastrantonio. (Curiously, *Class Action* also mentions the McCarthy hearings in a speech by Hackman's character about how he met his wife.)

What the two films really have in common is that both are relatively free of the kind of offensive excesses we so often see in movies. Neither film has any violence, there is no sex in either film, no nudity, and no drug abuse. Both films do have profanity, however, including that particular cuss word, the f-word, that is considered to be more offensive than any other by the rating board. And here's the irony: *Guilty by Suspicion* uses the word probably three times as often as *Class Action*, yet *Guilty by Suspicion* is rated PG-13 while *Class Action* is rated R.

I wrote at the time that, as borne out by national moviegoing statistics, it seemed unfortunate that some people would likely stay away from *Class Action* because of its R rating, but would feel fine about attending *Guilty by Suspicion*, simply because it is rated PG-13. And it brought to mind a number of other movies released before these two that are also rated R for no reason other than the use of the f-word a few times: *Ordinary People* (1980), *The Verdict* (1982), *The Milagro Beanfield War* (1988), and many others, none of which use profanity any more—and in some cases less—than *Guilty by Suspicion.*

None of this is meant to indict *Guilty By Suspicion*, which is a fine film and which, in its use of the expletive in question, doesn't come close to that word's ridiculous, over-the-top usage in such 1980s and '90s movies as *Beverly Hills Cop*, *Die Hard,* and their sequels, or anything by Quentin Tarantino (*Reservoir Dogs*, *Pulp Fiction*, etc.). *Guilty by Suspicion* uses the profanity logically and in angry, frustrated moments, rather than simply as another benign word in the vocabulary. But the fact remains that it is used a heck of a lot more in *Guilty by Suspicion* than *Class Action*, the latter being branded with an R, which is considered by some audiences to be the modern-day equivalent of Hester Prynne's "A".

Of course, discriminating audiences know how erratic the ratings can be, ranging from such disparate PG-13 films of the 1990s as *Awakenings*, a very clean film, save a couple of profanities, including the f-word spoken once, and *Dances with Wolves*, an Oscar-winner that is replete with violence, sex, and nudity. Then there was *King Ralph*, a film sold to children that featured a very raunchy scene in a strip joint, as well as vulgar and profane language, and the *Teenage Mutant Ninja Turtles* movies that were replete with comic violence—both rated PG. Not to mention that by virtue of its rating, *Class Action* was then categorized with such contemporary push-the-R-to-the-limit films as *The Silence of the Lambs* and *The Doors.*

No wonder parents are sometimes flummoxed by the rating system. Though, perhaps, not nearly as flummoxed as the members of the rating board.

In 2004, there was a little independent World War II drama titled *Saints and Soldiers,* which caused quite the brouhaha when it received an R rating and then appealed. Lots of movies get R ratings, of course, and not much is made of it. And many also go through the rating board's appeal process—sometimes editing the film, sometimes not—in order to have the rating reduced to PG-13. And you certainly never see it on the news.

However, *Saints and Soldiers* is an independent, made-in-Utah production with a largely Mormon cast and crew, and was, therefore, lumped (perhaps unfairly) with the "Mormon Cinema" movement of the early 2000s. So, the rating got a bit more national attention than it might have otherwise simply because the perceived audience—members of The Church of Jesus Christ of Latter-day Saints—is urged by church leaders to avoid R-rated movies.

Did the content, specifically wartime violence, really warrant a rating more harsh than some of its PG-13 competition at the time, say, *Master and Commander* or *Pearl Harbor* or the *Lord of the Rings* films or *Behind Enemy Lines* or the *Indiana Jones* sequels? If the rating didn't have such a negative stigma attached, perhaps, *Saints and Soldiers* would deserve an R—along with all the PG-13 movies named here. All are adult films with violence that could be quite disturbing to young children. But, when those films and so many others, earn PG-13s, it seems a bit silly for *Saints and Soldiers* to be singled out for an R.

I happened to see *Saints and Soldiers* before it was rated and my take was that it was simply too serious for the rating board. If the killings had had a comic kick or a fantasy element, the film might have earned a PG-13 automatically. True, the board operates under the mandate that movies be rated strictly on the basis of content, not quality. But I'm thinking that's a lot easier said than done.

So, if an Orc is beheaded or has limbs severed in *Lord of the Rings: The Return of the King,* with all the accompanying special effects, it is apparently less disturbing than it would be if a human is killed in the same manner. When, in *Raiders of the Lost Ark*, Indiana Jones guns down a swordsman in a marketplace and it gets a big laugh, or in the sequel *Indiana Jones and the Last Crusade*, when three Nazis are killed with one shot on a moving jeep and the audience laughs, that's apparently less disturbing for children. (Perhaps we can simply explain to impressionable kids that funny death is OK.)

It may be that *Saints and Soldiers* is simply too realistic. That is, the film is based on reality, and the characters are people we could know. And when they die or are mistreated, we feel it. The painful deaths are not funny, and there are repercussions. At the time, rating-board members never conveyed to filmmakers what precise content earned a particular rating, but I suspect the board was jumpy over two specific sequences in *Saints and Soldiers*:

- ★ The first opens the film, as Nazis casually shoot and kill a number of American prisoners for no apparent reason. They are in custody, they are unarmed, and they are shot down in a horrifying fashion. Disturbing? Yes. But strictly in terms of content, is it any more graphic than the above-named films? No.

- ★ The second comes when someone is shot in the leg and a medic tries to stop the bleeding. There are brief close-ups of the wound, and we see some blood gushing out. Disturbing? Yes. But more graphic than anything in the PG-13-rated *Pearl Harbor* or *Behind Enemy Lines*? No.

The appeal was successful and *Saints and Soldiers* went out with a PG-13 rating, but the fact that the process was necessary at all speaks again to ratings inconsistencies.

In 2007, a controversial R rating went to *There Will Be Blood*, an eccentric melodrama that won Daniel Day-Lewis his second Oscar for a brilliant performance as a reprehensible oilman over a twenty-nine-year period. Whatever your feelings about the movie, whether or not you can get into the story about the life and times of the miserly lead character, let's keep in mind that again, the rating board rates movies objectively and by virtue of content, regardless of subject matter.

Story, dialogue, character development, good guys, bad guys, upbeat, downbeat, political, or ideological agenda . . . none of this is supposed to matter. Violence, sex, nudity, language, drug use, smoking—the level of these things, how much, how graphic—are what members of CARA use to evaluate as they watch the movies they rate. Whether

Paul Dano and Daniel Day-Lewis in Paul Thomas Anderson's There Will Be Blood *(2007) —Miramax*

any of them loves, hates, or is indifferent to the film is irrelevant. At least in theory.

Not that the job can really be objective. Whatever they say, it's still a subjective business—especially in one area that has become a fairly recent addition to the above list: "thematic elements." Unlike the old days, when we often wondered why a movie had a rating, films now carry an explanation from the board specifying the content that earned each film its R or PG-13 or PG or G. *There Will Be Blood* is officially rated R for "some violence." That's it. If you watch the film, you'll see that it has a couple of scenes of accidental violence in the first half, and in the film's second half there are two murders. And none of these moments even approaches the level of violence in the average TV episode of prime-time television police procedurals.

So, should *There Will Be Blood* really be in the same R-rated category as the *Saw* and *Hostel* flicks? Or even its 2007 best-picture Oscar competition, *No Country for Old Men* or *Atonement* or *Michael Clayton*, all of which have content that is much more clearly in R-rated territory? If we were to discuss this philosophically, one could argue that *There Will Be Blood* is an adult film, with adult themes. It's dark and harsh and generally not a picture that impressionable youngsters should see anyway. So why not give it an R?

But the rating board can't start thinking like that. If it does, the board's members might have to rethink all those PG-13 movies that are adult films with adult themes and are generally not pictures that impressionable youngsters should see. And we can't have that.

In 2010, one of the year's most lauded and popular films was *The King's Speech*, the true story of England's King George VI (Colin Firth) who reluctantly assumes the throne, but is paralyzed by the thought of public speaking due to a pronounced stammer. The film chronicles his ascension and then his lessons with a most unorthodox speech therapist (Geoffrey Rush).

A key moment comes when the therapist instructs George to use profanity as a way of loosening up his voice and unlocking that stammer. He is at first reluctant to do so, but eventually begins cursing in a mild way. As he's encouraged to let go, George says the f-word several times, which seems to work. In the film's climactic sequence, he uses the technique again in a more subtle way before giving his first address over the radio.

These two profane sequences, played for laughs the first time and sentiment the second, account for the film's R rating. Harvey Weinstein, one of the executive producers, and whose company released *The King's Speech*, appealed for a PG-13, but was denied. The next year, he took the unusual step of having much of the profanity muted, re-submitted the film for a new rating and came away with a PG-13. This version was released theatrically, but did not do well at the box office, and as of this writing it has not surfaced on home video. The DVD and Blu-ray editions now available are the R-rated version.

It's interesting to note that in England, the language in the film initially earned *The King's Speech* a 15 rating, meaning that no one under fifteen years of age would be admitted. But on appeal there, the film received a 12A, meaning that no one under twelve may attend unless accompanied by an adult. The explanation says the film "contains strong language in a speech therapy context."

Unlike the five U.S. rating categories, the British movie-rating system has seven: R-18, which is strictly for pornography; 18, which is equivalent to America's R rating; 15, meaning no one under fifteen allowed; 12, meaning no one under twelve allowed; 12A, meaning no one under twelve allowed unless accompanied by an adult; PG, equivalent to the U.S. PG; and U, meaning Universal, nothing unsuitable for children.

In early 2012, another rating battle over language went public, again with movie mogul Harvey Weinstein, who this time complained loudly that the documentary *Bully*, which received an R, should have been PG-13. On National Public Radio he explained that in the film the f-word is spoken six times, and three of those usages are in the most important scene, in which a hidden camera captures schoolyard toughs harassing a victim.

Weinstein, whose company distributed *Bully*, formally appealed the R, but when the board dug in its heels, he announced that the film would go into theaters without a rating. Because the Weinstein Company is an independent organization and doesn't belong to the MPAA, its films are not required to carry ratings, although they usually do. But Weinstein, citing *Bully* as an important film that kids should be allowed to see, refused to accept the R.

In a last ditch effort, before the release date rolled around, *Bully* went back to CARA's appeals board, this time with three of the six usages bleeped — but the three in the scene cited by Weinstein remained intact. So the film was granted a PG-13. Now *Bully* is a PG-13 movie dropping the f-bomb three times, not counting bleeps; is this an unprecedented move on the part of CARA? Not by a long shot.

As mentioned above, there is a constant balance-of-power shift on the rating board because most of its eight-to-thirteen members serve only two or three years. With that kind of revolving-door membership, one year the board may be quite conservative and the next year it might be more liberal, resulting in periods when R or PG-13 movies may appear to be harsher or softer in terms of explicit content.

And once a movie is rated, unless it is to be submitted for a re-rating down the road, it stays rated. A well-known example is the 1976 classic *All the President's Men*, starring Robert Redford and Dustin Hoffman as Bob Woodward and Carl Bernstein, the journalists who uncovered the Watergate scandal in their investigative stories for the Washington Post. Their stories were then turned into a bestseller, and eventually became this film.

All the President's Men received a PG rating, even though the f-word is spoken some ten or eleven times. How'd that happen? Initially, *All the President's Men* received an R, but the studio appealed the rating, citing its historical importance to young people. The appeals board agreed and since there was no PG-13 rating at that time, the next non-R option was PG.

So if you rent *All the President's Men* today, you'll see that it carries a PG rating, and the language you hear in the film might surprise you. And that's actually true of quite a few 1970s and early 1980s movies.

In 1988, just four years after the PG-13 rating was put into use, two comedy/fantasies—Tim Burton and Michael Keaton's *Beetle Juice*, and Penny Marshall and Tom Hanks' *Big*—each snuck in the f-word once, but still managed to walk away with PG ratings.

And in the 1992 all-star caper comedy *Sneakers*, it's a bit of a shock to hear Sidney Poitier in a heated moment use the f-word in its even more obscene twelve-letter version. To my knowledge, no other PG-13 movie has ever gotten away with that.

The brouhaha over *Bully* was a bit surprising if only because the board was so adamant about not letting a PG-13 movie use the f-word more than once, even though it's been used at least twice in many PG-13 movies over the years, including *The Social Network*, the 2010 winner of the Oscar for best adapted screenplay.

In summer 2011, an article by *Los Angeles Times* writer Glenn Whipp went even further to suggest that a sort of "f-word creep" is apparent in PG-13 movies these days, as the expletive has shown up two or three times in a variety of films with that rating. Examples cited in the story included the 2010 films *The Tourist, Iron Man 2,* and *Wall Street: Money Never Sleeps*, and the 2011 films *The Adjustment Bureau* and *Transformers: Dark of the Moon.*

If these fiction films can get away with it, why did the rating board give such a hard time to *Bully*, which is as real life as movies get?

Really, though, the bigger question is for all these other films and especially *Iron Man 2* and *Transformers*, which are clearly aimed at young audiences: Why does the board allow that word to be in there at all?

Joan Graves, the head of CARA says in Whipp's story that if a couple of f-words are "innocuous" or far apart in the film or in the background and not emphatic, it makes a difference to board members. "All the raters are parents, and they're charged with rating a film the way they think a majority of American parents would rate the film. So that's the overriding focus."

As demonstrated by those involved, the rating board would have us believe that adults who go to the movies don't care about the ratings for themselves, only their children. But my experience suggests otherwise. There were many times during my movie-reviewing career when I heard from readers who wondered if certain upcoming films would carry an R rating, telling me that they hoped not because it was a movie they wanted to see, but if it was labeled with an R, they'd skip it.

Initially, when this started happening, I was surprised. But I gradually got used to it, and even began to make little side bets with myself about particular upcoming movies that seemed certain to generate calls. One I remember distinctly was *The Fugitive*, the 1993 thriller starring Harrison Ford and Tommy Lee Jones that became hugely popular, and which is arguably still the best movie ever made from a TV series. When *The Fugitive* received a PG-13, there seemed to be an almost audible sigh of relief from moviegoers all over.

It might seem like a no-brainer that filmmakers would like to avoid R ratings for general-audience movies, since statistically, with very few exceptions, PG-13 movies tend to out-perform R-rated movies at the box office. But there's no way to predict what the rating board will do.

When *A Perfect World*, a Clint Eastwood-directed film starring Kevin Costner and Eastwood, was scheduled for release in 1993, I happened to see a pre-rated print. After watching the film, I was sure it would be rated R, but to my surprise it received a PG-13. Then I read that Eastwood had to trim a few moments in the film before the rating board would change its mind about giving it an R. So, before reviewing it, I watched the film a second time and I couldn't tell what was cut. I know something was, but darned if I could spot it. To me it was the same film I expected to receive an R.

Perhaps, the biggest surprise to moviegoers during this time was the R rating given to *Schindler's List* in 1993. Not because the film doesn't deserve an R; it does. But because it was helmed by Steven Spielberg, and up to that time he had never directed a movie that received an R. In fact, eleven years earlier, in 1982, Spielberg was quoted by the *Los Angeles Times*, speaking of himself in the third person, as saying: "Steven Spielberg does not make R-rated movies."

Around the time Spielberg made that pronouncement, I was fortunate enough to snag an interview with him for two films he had scheduled for release at the time, *Poltergeist*, which Spielberg produced and Tobe Hooper directed (although rumors at the time suggested Spielberg had a hand in directing as well), and *E.T.: The Extra-Terrestrial*, which Spielberg directed and has always called the most personal of his films. So I asked Spielberg if he had really made that statement to the *L.A. Times*. "Yes, I said that," he admitted. "Because I'm this parochial prude. If I did an erotic love scene, it would have to be off-camera. Or if I did it on camera, it would have to be under the covers."

Of course, that was more than a decade before *Schindler* came along. And even when he made that early pronouncement it wasn't precisely true. Unless "make" is defined as "directs." Spielberg also produces many movies that he does not direct, and in 1980 the raunchy comedy *Used Cars* carried his name. But that was his only R-rated production prior to *Schindler's List*. Although, since we're picking at nits, he also acted in an R-rated movie in 1980, *The Blues Brothers*, in which he makes a brief cameo appearance.

Still, to this day, Spielberg continues to churn out mostly PG and PG-13 movies. The only R-rated pictures he has produced since *Schindler's List* are those he has also directed: *Amistad* (1997), *Saving Private Ryan* (1998), and *Munich* (2005), along with a pair of World War II films directed by Clint Eastwood, *Flags of Our Fathers*, and *Letters from Iwo Jima* (both 2006).

One of the things I was charged with when I became the full-time movie critic at the *Deseret News* was to see that every commercial film that came through Salt Lake City, some 250 annually, was not only reviewed, but also that the rating for each was thoroughly explained. There had never been a full-time movie critic at the paper before, and, as movies were getting more and more graphic in terms of content, the newspaper's owners wanted the readers to be as fully informed as possible.

This didn't affect my opinion writing; I still called 'em as I saw 'em. But, I had to pay strict attention to the content, even as I was watching for artistic and entertainment value. It required note taking, sometimes in detail, and, though I never went in for statistics, counting offensive words or detailing every specific offensive moment— how could I do that and still evaluate the film on other levels?—I tried to

Val Kilmer as Jim Morrison with his band in Oliver Stone's The Doors *(1991) —TriStar*

help the moviegoers who read my reviews to be educated on every level so they could choose wisely, and that included knowing if they were going to be assaulted on some level.

No other papers were really doing this at the time, at least not as thoroughly. A few years later, however, everyone was doing it, and eventually, even CARA was doing it. (I'm not trying to take credit for this, by the way; detailing potentially offensive content was actually instituted by the *Deseret News* before I became the film critic. But up to this time editors had relied on wire services to provide what was usually limited, and sometimes incorrect, information.)

Ever since its inception in 1968, CARA has been publishing a weekly bulletin that announces which movies have been rated and what that rating is. But during the first couple of decades there were no descriptions about any film's content. That changed in 1991, when the bulletins suddenly began to include a brief explanation of each R rating. But only for R-rated movies.

In those first few months, I took note of some of the explanations. Bruce Willis' *Hudson Hawk* was "rated R for language." Spike Lee's *Jungle Fever* was "rated R for sensuality, strong language, drug content, and for violence." Madonna's concert documentary *Truth or Dare* was "rated R for sensuality, violence, and some language." Oliver Stone's *The Doors* was "rated R for heavy drug content, and for strong sexuality and language."

When this change was first announced, I had thought it might make my job easier. I could review a movie without having to take such specific notice of all the potentially objectionable content because the bulletins would provide that information. But those four films were among many that clued me in rather quickly that CARA's explanations would be woefully incomplete. There was no mention of the enormous amount of violence in *Hudson Hawk*, the violence and nudity in *The Doors*, nor the nudity in *Jungle Fever* and *Truth or Dare*. And though the words "sensuality" and "sexuality" were apparently intended to encompass nudity, there are nonsexual nude scenes in both *Truth or Dare* and *The Doors*.

And since only R-rated movies carried explanations, a number of PG and PG-13 movies that contained extreme violence or wall-to-wall profanity or sex or nudity held some surprises for the moviegoer. Examples in 1991 were the PG-rated Disney picture *The Rocketeer*, which is quite violent, and the nudity in *Drop Dead Fred*, *FX 2*, and *Only the Lonely*, all of which were rated PG-13.

At the time, I wrote that while to some this might seem like nit-picking, we need to remember that the rating board is charged with performing its duty for parents, to help them guide their children to and from certain films. It's hard enough for parents to second-guess the ratings when they are nothing more than a series of letters on a poster, I wrote, especially since they've always been inconsistent and seemingly arbitrary.

Then, here came explanations for R-rated movies, but they were so murky that the change hardly seemed designed to build faith in the system. If the members of the board didn't notice violence or nudity, no wonder so many movies seem to carry the wrong ratings. And how did these explanations help parents with children, since their children weren't supposed to be seeing R-rated movies?

Eventually, the board saw the wisdom of explaining all the ratings, not just the Rs. And that's the way it is today, with PGs and PG-13s, as well as Rs, having a brief explanation of why the film has a certain rating . . . and the details still seem murky. Oh, sometimes it gets specific enough to provide some concrete information, as with this one for *The Girl with the Dragon Tattoo*: "Rated R for brutal violent content including rape and torture, strong sexuality, graphic nudity, and language." That's pretty detailed.

But then along comes another that makes you wonder if they even saw the movie, such as this one for *Bridesmaids* (2011): "Rated R for some strong sexuality, and language throughout." I know people who walked out of *Bridesmaids* before it was half over and they say it wasn't for sexuality or language, but for all the gross-out humor, including bodily functions portrayed in such a disgusting manner that even the most repulsive movies that have gone before pale in comparison.

Filmmakers and studios got their feathers ruffled in late 2009 when it was announced that the adult comedy *It's Complicated* had been rated R by CARA. The late-in-life romantic comedy starring Meryl Streep, Steve Martin, and Alec Baldwin became the subject of controversy due to the reason for the rating as much as for the rating itself. Not that anyone knew for sure at the time exactly what that reason was, since CARA never reveals anything about its decisions beyond the terse description included with the rating label. But then, Hollywood never did let the facts get in the way of a good story.

In the case of *It's Complicated*, the R rating was for "some drug content and sexuality." Terse enough for you? The "drug content" responsible for the rating is easy enough to figure out since the only drug used in the film is marijuana during a comic sequence that has Streep and Martin's characters indulging in a joint on their way to a party, causing their inhibitions to fall away as predictable hijinks ensue. The "sexuality," a secondary reason for the rating, would have to be Streep and Baldwin's post-coital heavy breathing and some dialogue (the scene depicted on the film's poster), along with a shot of Baldwin's backside. There's no other sex or nudity in the film, though there's plenty of sex talk and innuendo, along with some profanity.

The controversy revolved around whether *It's Complicated* deserved its R rating, and the discussion, led by the *Los Angeles Times* and the *New York Times*—along with that old devil, the blogosphere—was indeed complicated. Again, because the rating board never extrapolates on its one-line explanations, the news reports cited off-the-record comments, allegedly from MPAA members in the know, suggesting that the R rating had nothing to do with sexuality and everything to do with the lack of consequences for smoking a reefer. Which is surprising since an illegal high is hardly unprecedented in PG-13 movies. For that matter, the sexual content is a lot less raunchy than most PG-13 sex comedies, many of which involve teens. Still, when the studio appealed, it lost. The R rating stood.

An interesting comparison is the family film *Whale Rider* (2002), which many people in and outside the film industry felt should be rated PG. It was rated PG-13 "for brief language and a momentary drug reference." The film does have a few vulgar or profane phrases, but the tipping point was apparently the "drug reference," when the camera briefly shows a man sleeping with a bag of what appears to be marijuana and a drug pipe on his chest, which he quickly tucks away when he is awakened, and no one is shown smoking or otherwise taking drugs. So would *Whale Rider* now earn an R rating?

The question everyone was asking about *It's Complicated* was, is this a throwback to the movie censorship of the 1930s, when crimes without consequences could not be depicted? If so, perhaps we would no longer see PG-13 movies that depict underage drinking or teen sex or marijuana smoking or prescription-drug abuse or any other crime or act of violence . . . unless the offender is duly punished. The complaints were valid—there did seem to be a double standard, and the R rating for *It's Complicated* was certainly not fair in comparison to so many other films. So the newspapers' (and blogosphere's) arguments were sound . . . as far as they went.

But instead of all those complaints about *It's Complicated* being rated R, the ire should have been directed at all those other movies being rated PG-13. Let's take another 2009 movie, the PG-13-rated sex comedy *Couples Retreat*, a film that is loaded with raunchy dialogue and scenes depicting sexual arousal. How is this appropriate for thirteen-, fourteen-, fifteen-year-olds? And there are many other 2009 examples—*The Proposal*, *He's Just Not That Into You*, *An Education*, *Obsessed*, *(500) Days of Summer*—all adult films with sexual content that received PG-13 ratings.

What seems to have been lost in this discussion is the reason for the existence of the ratings, which the MPAA defines as a gauge for parents as to what is appropriate for various age levels. Thus, a PG-13 rating means a film's content is OK for a child of thirteen or older. But how is ANY sexuality appropriate for a thirteen-year-old? Why is there so much sexual content in that year's second-biggest moneymaker, *Transformers: Revenge of the Fallen* (which also has a marijuana joke, by the way), and why wasn't that film threatened with an R rating? Clearly, it's because the *Transformers* sequel would not have been the year's second-biggest moneymaker had it been rated R.

I know, I know, the MPAA claims that there is never any undue studio pressure or influence on the rating board and . . . oh look, a flying pig. Hey, it's no secret that, generally speaking, PG-13 movies earn more money than R-rated movies. So, with a few obvious exceptions—*The Hangover* (2009) and *Saw VI* (2007) and *Bridesmaids* and others purposely sold as "hard-R" movies—the studios and filmmakers don't want R ratings. R ratings can cut into profits. Mind you, that doesn't prompt any of them to eliminate the R-rated elements. It just prompts them to complain when they receive an R rating.

It's Complicated is an adult movie. It should be rated R. But all of these other films are also very adult. And they should be rated R as well.

Before concluding this discussion of the R rating, I should point out that although the NC-17 rating goes largely unused these days, it's an empty category simply because movies that belong there usually end up being released either as an unrated movie or with an R rating after a few trims to satisfy the board. And those trims are most often very brief edits, just a few seconds of the film snipped away before it is resubmitted to the board for another shot at receiving an R.

To receive ratings, movies are submitted to CARA's primary rating board, a panel of parents hired to watch films daily and then decide what rating each film deserves. But for appeals, it's a different board made up of fifteen film-industry executives. Sound like a conflict of interest? Yes, and that's been pointed out to CARA and the MPAA many times, but it has always fallen on deaf ears.

At least nine members of the appeals board must be present, and whether a rating is overturned is decided by a two-thirds vote. Most movies that are appealed either want to go from R to PG-13, or from NC-17 to R. And, again, money is the motivator since R films generally earn less at the box office than PG-13s, and NC-17s have a difficult time getting into mainstream theaters at all, much less having a successful run.

During the summer of 2012, the picture that was trying to lose its NC-17 rating in favor of an R was *Killer Joe*, a thriller from filmmaker William Friedkin, whose most popular pictures are *The Exorcist* (1973) and *The French Connection* (1971). By all accounts *Killer Joe* is over-the-top on several levels, dealing with unpleasant characters in horrifying circumstances, and features violence that is extremely graphic and stomach-churning.

After receiving an NC-17 for "graphic disturbing content involving violence and sexuality, and a scene of brutality," *Killer Joe*'s rating was appealed, but the board declined to make the change. According to the *Los Angeles Times*, David Dinerstein, whose LD Distribution released the film, told the board, "We strongly feel that *Killer Joe* was arbitrarily and unfairly rated NC-17," and he cited such other R-rated movies as *The Girl with the Dragon Tattoo* (2011), *Black Swan* (2010), *A History of Violence* (2005), and *Pulp Fiction* (1994) as examples of movies that "contain comparable adult material and received less restrictive R ratings, as well as *The Hunger Games* (2012), which features kids killing their peers and is rated PG-13."

But his argument did not motivate the desired result. Since LD Distribution is not a member of the MPAA, the film could have gone out unrated rather than try to earn bookings with an NC-17, but the distributor ultimately chose to retain the NC-17 and capitalize on it as the film was marketed to the art-house circuit, which is generally more tolerant of such pictures.

Let's look at the specific definition of the NC-17 rating as posted on CARA's website: "These are films that the Rating Board believes parents would consider patently too adult for their children. No children will be admitted. NC-17 does not necessarily mean 'obscene' or 'pornographic' and should not be construed as a negative judgment on the content of the film. The rating simply signals that the content is appropriate only for an adult audience. An NC-17 rating can be based on violence, sex, aberrational behavior, drug abuse, or any other element that most parents would consider too strong, and therefore, off-limits for viewing by their children."

Sounds like a lot of PG-13 movies to me, but, of course, an NC-17 really means material that is repellent above and beyond even the most explicit R-rated standard.

The NC-17 was established in 1990, and the first film released with that rating was *Henry & June*, a major-studio release based on the diaries of Anais Nin about her open sexual relationship with author Henry Miller and his wife June in 1930s France. It is an explicit film but in 1990 I wrote that "there is nothing here that has not been seen in countless R-rated movies. Why then did it get an NC-17 instead of an R? Probably because more screen time than usual is devoted to the sex scenes—not because those scenes are any more explicit."

In other words, though it inaugurated the NC-17 rating, *Henry & June* is not that far removed from an R-rated movie of the time. But the point is that this rating was not intended as one to corral pornography, but rather to collect movies that kids shouldn't see. I also wrote in my 1990 review, "NC-17 movies will likely be a bit harder in content than R-rated movies, but the point of the new rating is that it automatically locks out children. When accompanied by a parent or guardian, kids can get into any R-rated movie. But NC-17 means no children under the age of seventeen will be admitted, whether or not someone older buys them a ticket."

If the studios, filmmakers and members of the rating board today would use the NC-17 as it is defined by the CARA website, they could easily put many movies that are now rated R into that category and it would just be another, more harsh rating that indicates a film is for adults only. But as long as it is associated with obscenity, that's not going to happen.

On the other hand, if filmmakers would simply make their movies and tell their stories, and stop pushing the limits of audience tolerance, if they would make movies with artful subtlety instead of graphic visuals designed to be rougher and tougher and more shocking than those that came before, it wouldn't even be an issue.

Chapter 4

PG-13 RAPIDLY BECOMES R-LITE

The R rating is meant to warn parents that kids should not attend, but a lot of adults take on that warning for themselves, as validated by a May 2012 *Los Angeles Times* story that suggests the PG-13 is the most attractive rating for audiences, and the most appealing for movie studios because it's the rating with the biggest box-office track record. The story points out that the six highest-grossing movies of all time worldwide carry that rating (its source being Box Office Mojo—www.boxofficemojo.com—a website that tracks movie stats).

A few months after that story was published, the number rose from six to seven as *The Avengers* joined the list. And to break it down further, Box Office Mojo's list of the top hundred biggest moneymakers worldwide contains only three R-rated movies. The vast majority are PG-13, with G and PG films filling out the list.

The *L.A. Times* story also states that PG-13 films account "for 35.1 percent of all movies rated in the U.S., but 54.4 percent of the box office."

And it goes on to say, "Though it's easy to assume that the PG-13 rating chiefly helps parents decide what their kids can—and can't—see, it now is used by some adults in choosing what they should see themselves, particularly those uncomfortable with graphic sex, violence, and language." Examples cited were *Hope Springs* and *The Best Exotic Marigold Hotel*, both about people in their twilight years, obviously not themes that would appeal to teens—yet both films pursued, and received, PG-13 ratings.

The *Times* also pointed to inconsistencies in the rating system and what triggers an R. Two 2012 films cited as examples were *The Good Doctor*, which, according to the board, contains "thematic material, disturbing situations, and some crude sexual content," and *The Perks of Being a Wallflower*, with "mature thematic material, drug and alcohol use, sexual content including references, and a fight—all involving teens." Both films earned R ratings, then appealed, and, according to the *Times*, "were changed to PG-13 marks on appeal without the filmmakers altering a frame."

When the PG-13 rating came into being in 1984, it was often referred to by industry insiders as "the Spielberg rating," referring to Steven Spielberg. The renowned filmmaker had been championing a rating that would fall in between PG and R because he rightly felt that there were a lot of movies that clearly shouldn't be rated R, but which were also, clearly, too adult for a PG. In fact, some of his own early movies fell into that category, and it was perhaps the battles he waged with CARA over *Jaws* and *Raiders of the Lost Ark* that emboldened his argument. That's right, the rating board initially considered giving an R to each of those films, but before the ratings were officially handed out, Spielberg successfully talked down the board members and managed to swing PG ratings for both films.

Answering questions on the subject when I interviewed him in 1982 as he was promoting *E.T.: The Extra-Terrestrial*, which he directed, and *Poltergeist*, which he produced—two years before the PG-13 was adopted—Spielberg said, "I have never been able to get involved in a movie that on the surface had gratuitous violence or gratuitous sexual encounters or gratuitous language. It just doesn't make sense." He admitted, however, that the PG-rated *Jaws* and *Raiders* were certainly a bit rough for very young children, but argued that it is a cinematic tradition to make films for kids that scare them.

CARA did stamp an R rating on *Poltergeist,* which surprised Spielberg. Convinced that the rating was overly harsh, he asked for a re-hearing, then went before the appeals board and argued his case, using as a comparative example the first movie that scared him as a child. "I was terrified in *Snow White,*" Spielberg explained. "I said (to the board), 'Walt Disney has terrified children for thirty years. Please don't blame me for putting kids in jeopardy. Disney has done it better than I ever will.' And we won and got the PG for *Poltergeist.* "

On the other hand, Spielberg conceded that he purposely added some foul language to the PG-rated *E.T.: The Extra-Terrestrial* for the purpose of avoiding a G. "It (the G rating) seems to say to people that it's too young for adolescents." This is an argument still used today by family-oriented filmmakers who are leery of G ratings. Ever wonder why so many modern animated movies for children are rated PG instead of G, and seem to have gratuitous language or body-function gags or sexual innuendoes that seem inappropriate for children's movies? There's your answer.

Spielberg said in 1982 that the rating system is good—because it's the only one we have and is better than state-by-state censorship—but he added that he would also like to see an interim rating between R and PG. "I think there should be something called R-13 or R-12, which essentially means that someone over twelve can see a picture unaccompanied by a parent or guardian, (and) under twelve they must adhere to the same rule that applies to the R rating, only instead of seventeen, it's age twelve. *Poltergeist* would be an R-12." From Steven Spielberg's mouth to Jack Valenti's ear.

As if to press the issue, in summer 1984 Spielberg had another pair of releases that brought an even greater outcry from critics and parents because they seemed to push the PG rating to the limit: *In-*

diana Jones and the Temple of Doom, which was much darker than its predecessor, *Raiders of the Lost Ark*, and the horror-satire *Gremlins*, which was also dark and violent (and with a character relating an especially not-for-children story about Santa Claus). Whether or not it was aimed specifically at a youth audience, the film, nonetheless, attracted the attention of children who found its puppet-like title creatures appealing in television advertising. (Movies still attract the wrong audience due to less-than-honest advertising with characters that, on the surface, would seem to appeal to children, as with the 2012 R-rated fantasy-farce *Ted*, discussed in Chapter 9.)

It was pretty obvious to everyone at the time that *Temple of Doom* and *Gremlins* were awfully strong for PG-rated movies.

My 1984 review of *Indiana Jones and the Temple of Doom* noted, "Like *Raiders*, *Indiana Jones* is *very* violent. A man's heart is torn out of his chest while he remains alive, various people are shot, fall from great heights, are devoured by crocodiles, and die in other sundry ways. And though there are no snakes or tarantulas, there are such delights as cockroaches galore, vampire bats, and the eating of disgusting Indian delicacies (such as live eels) to raise your adrenalin. In other words, heed the warning below the PG rating: '. . . may be too intense for younger children.' " (I think I forgot to mention the serving of monkey brains.)

And of *Gremlins*, I wrote: ". . . before you pack up your little ones for this picture, be advised that the film goes from a benign sweetness in the *E.T.* vein to a horror-movie motif, with the nasty mogwai resembling Muppets going berserk." And in conclusion, I reiterated: "Rated PG, but decidedly not for young children, being loaded with violence."

In an interview with *Vanity Fair* in January 2008, Spielberg talked again about the PG-13 rating and his role in making it happen. "I remember calling Jack Valenti and suggesting to him that we need a rating between R and PG . . . I suggested, 'Let's call it PG-13 or PG-14, depending on how you want to design the slide rule,' and Jack came back to me and said, 'We've determined that PG-13 would be the right age for that temperature of movie.' So I've always been very proud that I had something to do with that rating."

Indiana Jones and the Temple of Doom came out in May 1984, followed by *Gremlins* in June, and by early August, the PG-13 was not only in place, but managed to have a film in general theatrical release: *Red Dawn*, a thriller about a Soviet invasion on U.S. soil and a group of teenagers that attempts to thwart the attack. (A *Red Dawn* remake was released in November 2012.)

By 1984 standards, *Red Dawn* is a pretty violent film, and, naturally, has its share of foul language, so it seemed to address the main complaint about PG movies that appeared to be too adult—violence displayed on the screen in a manner that seems too strong for the more family-oriented PG rating. Still, PG-13—emphasis on the "13"—suggests that material contained in a movie with that rating is fine for all teens, a point that seems completely lost on both the rating board and the filmmakers. And *Red Dawn* is another film that attracted a youth audience, since teenagers are, after all, the film's heroes.

And it wasn't long after the implementation of the PG-13 that moviemakers began to see it as the go-to rating for "adult" movies that the studios, and movie writers and directors, did not want to see with the more restrictive R—that is, restrictive in terms of keeping out the biggest moviegoing demographic, teenagers, and more important, lowering the odds for box-office success. Fast-forward to 2012 and it's not uncommon for studios to have filmmakers sign contracts guaranteeing a movie will be delivered with a PG-13 rating. If CARA gives such a movie an R, the director is then required to appeal for the desired rating, even if it means trimming something from the film.

By 1984, there was little question that the ratings system had become relaxed over the years, with gore, violence, sex, nudity, profanity, and vulgarity being allowed with more and more abundance in PG-rated films, and each of those same elements being pushed to the limits in many films rated R. Yet, with movies as clean as *Ordinary People* and *The Verdict* carrying the same R rating as the incredibly raunchy *Porky's* or the extremely violent *Friday the 13th*, and with the same PG rating applied equally to the squeaky clean musical *Annie* and the violent *Raiders of the Lost Ark* and the sexual James Bond picture *Never Say Never Again*, people often went in worrying: Will I be grossed-out or embarrassed if I bring a date, or will we be comfortable if we take our children? And as they left the theaters, some were asking the same question in reverse: Why in the world are these softer films rated R and these rougher films rated PG?

This became an even greater concern in the early 1980s due to the rise in home-video availability. Videocassettes of popular movies were starting to flood the marketplace, mostly for rent at that time (the cost factor precluded the average fan from purchasing films for home libraries), and the video boxes carried the film's theatrical rating. In the

Harrison Ford in Steven Spielberg's Indiana Jones and the Temple of Doom *(1984) —Paramount*

comfort of their own homes, parents were discovering rather quickly that just because a movie carried a PG didn't mean kids should be allowed watch it.

I'm a bit embarrassed to admit that I had an experience like this myself when the PG-rated *Raiders of the Lost Ark* was released on video for the first time in the late 1980s and my children were clamoring to see it. *Indiana Jones and the Temple of Doom* would have been an automatic "no," but at the time my memory of *Raiders*, some seven or eight years after its 1981 debut, was that it was lighter and more family-friendly than its sequel and might be OK. My children ranged in age at that time from my youngest boy, a toddler, to my oldest girl, in her early teens.

So, I rented *Raiders* and it wasn't on very long before I began to question my decision, as the movie proved to be replete with foul language, and was very violent and scary in places. I managed to spirit the younger kids out of the room before the ghostly creatures and melting faces appeared toward the end, but I regretted allowing any of them to watch it at their tender ages. If the movie critic who complains about such things all the time can forget about the "bad parts," so can any parent. And that's what we tend to do, especially with films we really enjoy. (I should have dug up my old review and read my own warnings.)

The words of Jack Valenti came back to haunt me: "Only parents are qualified to make personal family judgments about their children's viewing habits." And sometimes we have to learn from our mistakes.

When the PG-13 was finally put into place in 1984, there were mixed reactions nationally, but the response was mostly positive, even from those critical of the ratings system.

Roger Ebert, movie critic for the *Chicago Sun-Times*, and at the time co-host with Gene Siskel (movie critic for the *Chicago Tribune*) of a popular movie-review television program, praised the new rating. "It's a good idea to create PG-13 as a way of giving the original

PG category its teeth back. In the last analysis, as Valenti points out, enforcement of the whole ratings system is really up to the nation's parents. PG-13 will give them useful information. In some cases, it will alert them to movies not suitable for kids under thirteen. In a lot more cases, I suspect, what it will really signify is a movie not suitable for viewing by adults."

David Sterritt, movie critic for the *Christian Science Monitor* until his retirement in 2005, said in 1984 that the PG-13 was a step in the right direction, adding, "But the real answer to protection problems is for parents to take the PG initials at their face value—to read reviews, check with friends and neighbors, phone theaters with specific questions, and generally provide the 'parental guidance' that's needed. If parents shouldered more of the guidance burden themselves, they could expect less from—and be better served by—the shorthand of the rating system." (Today, of course, we would suggest checking informative websites rather than trying to phone theaters, which likely offer nothing more than recordings with showtimes.)

The capper was an item reported in a 1984 *USA Today* article. Although *Red Dawn* was the first PG-13 movie to go into release, a little picture titled *The Zoo Gang* was actually the first to receive the new rating. And one of the filmmakers wasn't happy about it, publicly protesting, "You don't change the rules at halftime of the Super Bowl." Producer Kerry Hersch said, "The rating shouldn't apply to films that were already finished [before the PG-13 was in place]." Hersch said her film received the rating for "sexual innuendo," an inaccurate perception since it was intended as a family film about teenagers starting a dance club.

Hersch's allegation that her movie undeservedly received the PG-13 rating for "sexual innuendo" was either speculation on her part or information that came from an industry insider who claimed to know, since the CARA board at that time declined to offer up reasons for its ratings. My 1985 review of the comedy cites "violence, profanity, and vulgarity." By today's standards, *The Zoo Gang* would probably receive a PG-13 just for the young boy who's always smoking or the teenagers who are drinking alcohol. There is also considerable foul language, some violence, and, yes, some innuendo.

The Zoo Gang is a largely forgotten movie today. Despite a videotape release in 1991, it has never made its way to DVD. But the film's place in history is secure as the first to receive a PG-13 rating, awarded in the summer of 1984. But because the movie didn't make its way into theaters for nearly a year, showing up with little-to-no fanfare in June 1985, it is *Red Dawn* that gets all the attention as the "first" PG-13 movie.

One could argue, and many do, that today's action movies are not a lot different than the shows our parents and grandparents (and great-grandparents) watched as children in the olden days, with guys in white hats shooting and killing guys in black hats in a steady stream of western, gangster, and exotic adventure movies. Except that the films were usually in black and white, color being less common until the 1960s, and nobody swore. In addition, the killings, however many there might be in a given film, were more restrained. Before the "realistic" revolution of the 1960s, whether they were thrillers, action pictures, westerns, science fiction yarns, or police procedurals, whenever someone was shot there was often no blood, and just as often there wasn't even a bullet hole in the fabric of their clothing.

That began to change during the 1950s and into the 1960s, but the gloves really came off with *Bonnie and Clyde* in 1967 and *The Wild Bunch* in 1969. Although patently adult in its themes, in terms of content *Bonnie and Clyde* doesn't really go too far until the climax, a famous sequence that has the title characters being gunned down by police, and that hail of machine-gun fire is quite graphic as it tears at their clothing and flesh (and their car), causing a gruesome dance of death, with blood flying everywhere, much of it unspooling on-screen in slow-motion. This was quite shocking to mainstream 1967 audience members who had never seen anything quite like it on the screen before.

Just two years later, *The Wild Bunch* took advantage of the doors opened by *Bonnie and Clyde* and featured blood and gore aplenty, from the opening sequence forward, to such a degree that it was also considered shocking at the time. This was a signal of what was to come and the ratings on both films tell a story of just how arbitrary CARA's decisions can be.

The Wild Bunch was rated R in 1969 but *Bonnie and Clyde* was made before ratings, and, therefore, initially went into theaters with no rating. Perhaps to cash in on the success of *The Wild Bunch*, Warner Bros., the studio that financed and released both movies, began to prepare *Bonnie and Clyde* for a re-release in 1969 and so submitted it for its first rating. The film came back with an M, the rating that would evolve just a couple of years later into PG. Early home-video releases of *Bonnie and Clyde* labeled the film "unrated," apparently feeling the "M" would go unrecognized. But in 2007, when the film was going to be reissued on DVD in a couple of multiple-disc editions, it was resubmitted to CARA. The studio expected the M to simply become PG, but instead CARA gave it an R. For the first time, forty years after its initial release, *Bonnie and Clyde* became an R-rated movie.

Similarly, in the early 1990s, as *The Wild Bunch* was about to be re-released in theaters in a restored, expanded "director's cut," the film was resubmitted to CARA because the newly edited version now differed somewhat from the original, which had been rated R more than twenty years earlier. CARA rules require that if a film is altered in any way from its originally rated form it must be reviewed by the board again before it can go out with the rating. This new version had ten minutes more footage, but since none of that footage included violence, Warner Bros. asked for the re-rating merely as a formality. But the studio got a bit of a shock when *The Wild Bunch* came back with an NC-17. This essentially stopped the planned theatrical re-release in its tracks until the studio was eventually able to successfully argue for and receive another R rating.

Every year it seems some movie is stamped with an R that feels undeserved according to the filmmakers or the studios—even the general public. Early in 2012 it was *Bully*, as described in Chapter 3. The year before it was the best-picture Oscar-winner *The King's Speech* and the critical darling *Win Win*, a lower-budget independent production. Both were rated R for language, specifically a few usages of the f-word.

The question was asked in many circles: Should those films be in the same rating category as the *Scream* and *Saw* franchises or *Bridesmaids* and *The Hangover*? On the other hand, to name movies released in 2011, around the same time as *The King's Speech* and *Win Win*, should the very violent vampire yarn *Priest* be rated PG-13? Or *Fast Five*, with its enormous body count of both bad guys and cops, along with a surprising amount of sexual dialogue, mostly anatomical wisecracks by the chauvinistic male characters? We all love a good action flick, but should they receive a rating that makes it easier for kids to see the bodies pile up as the heroes demonstrate not the least bit of remorse—and in fact, may even make a joke?

We can blame the latter on James Bond. Whether he was the first movie hero/anti-hero to drop a bon mot upon blowing someone away is arguable, but there is no question that he popularized it. Bond's post-killing quips are quick, sometimes spoken to a witness or investigator—or just as an aside to himself—as he hastily departs from the crime scene. And they are usually in the form of a pun related to the method of death or in reference to the victim.

The early sixties introduction of this British agent with a double-0 license to kill also pushed at what had been allowed under the Production Code regarding on-screen deaths. Up to this time, when a good guy killed a bad guy, it was an act of self-defense. And that's also true of most of Bond's killings . . . but not all. His license to kill, after all, makes him tantamount to a sanctioned assassin. Kill whom you must with no pesky criminal prosecution to worry about. Once in awhile his killings are quite cold-blooded, but the audience lets him get away with it because the villain is so heinous or because Bond makes a joke that diffuses the act. Under other circumstances it might look like murder, but audience sympathy remains with Bond because he has that double-0 caveat, he's charming and funny, and the bad guy is just so bad.

Plus, the Bond films are replete with sexual imagery, scantily clad women, and characters with salacious names. This potent combination of sex and violence was new in the 1960s. And while it, arguably, may make for enjoyable entertainment, the question remains, is it really good for our children? Or should James Bond movies be rated R?

The first 007 flick, *Dr. No* (1962), had relatively few such quips, but then they seemed to exponentially increase with *From Russia With Love* (1963), *Goldfinger* (1964), *Thunderball* (1965), and *You Only Live Twice* (1967), all of which were made before the rating system was initiated, but which received PGs for later theatrical reissues. The first Bond film to be rated PG-13 was *Licence to Kill* (1989), and ever since the Bond movies have all received PG-13s, right up to the latest, *Skyfall* (2012).

There were plenty of espionage dramas before Bond—from a wide array of World War II propaganda films to several Alfred Hitchcock thrillers. But the enormous popularity of Bond altered the genre in tone, ushering in an explosion of lighthearted spy/caper flicks, mixing violence and jokes about killing and sex, from the 1960s forward. Some are direct spoofs and others are merely frothy romps that go their own way—*The Liquidator*, *Where the Spies Are*, *A Man Could Get Killed.*

A few were so popular that they spawned film franchises of their own, however briefly—Michael Caine as Harry Palmer (five movies, beginning with *The Ipcress File*), James Coburn as Derek Flint (two, *Our Man Flint*), Dean Martin as Matt Helm (four, *The Silencers*), and the more recent *Austin Powers* comedies with Mike Myers (four and counting). Many TV series also followed, with gimmicks, gadgets, and style owing much to Bond, from *The Man from U.N.C.L.E.* and *I Spy* to *Alias* and *Nikita*. (Although, it must be said that a few more serious, low-key, gimmick-free spy melodramas still occasionally crop up, from 1965's *The Spy Who Came in From the Cold* to 2012's *Tinker Tailor Soldier Spy*.)

Making jokes after committing an act of violence isn't exclusive to spy films. It's also a staple of PG-13 heroes like Indiana Jones, and all the way up to several characters in the 2012 mega-blockbuster *The Avengers*. And it also holds for such R-rated anti-heroes as *Dirty Harry* (Clint

Eastwood) and John McClane (Bruce Willis in the *Die Hard* movies). Making snarky jokes after killing or injuring someone has become one of the standard clichés for American action films, whatever the genre. But there's no question that it also trivializes violence and death. And what are we to make of the fourth McClane movie, *Live Free or Die Hard* (2007) receiving a PG-13 rating? That was not the case for *A Good Day to Die Hard* (2013), which reverted back to the R rating.

The model, established by the James Bond pictures, of adult action movies pursuing a PG-13 rating in order to reach a larger, younger audience—whether or not the film is appropriate for that audience—is becoming more and more common. The fourth *Die Hard* isn't unique. In 1993, *RoboCop 3* earned a PG-13 after two R-rated entries in that series. And many other franchises have pursued the PG-13 from the get-go. Aside from the obvious superhero examples—*Superman*, *Batman*, *Spider-Man*, *Iron Man*, etc.—such multiple-film franchises as *The Bourne Identity*, *Ghost Rider*, *Hellboy*, and *The Hunger Games*, as well as one-shot pictures like *Salt* and *Lockout*, are violent PG-13 films that hardly seem like kiddie fare.

Whether the amount of violence, sex, and/or language is really toned down much in those pictures is up for debate. Board members, although they are told not to, could be comparing them to R-rated movies they are exposed to on a daily basis and simply assigning PG-13s because the content isn't as harsh.

Let's look at *RoboCop* as an example. The first two films in the *RoboCop* series are R-rated movies with extreme gory, bloody violence. The first *RoboCop* came out in 1987 and was so violent that the rating board gave the film an X. And that X-rated version was so harsh that it took twelve trips to the appeals board to earn an R. That is, the film received an X rating eleven more times before the board capitulated and reduced the rating. Remember that board members have to view the entire film on each appeal before deciding on a rating, which has long made me wonder if they really felt *RoboCop* deserved the R or they just didn't want to have to sit through it a thirteenth time.

Even after all of that, the amount and graphic depiction of violence in the R-rated *RoboCop* was still shocking for mainstream audiences at the time. This wasn't a grindhouse exploitation film playing on the bottom of a drive-in double-bill, it was a major-studio release being sold heavily to the mainstream through newspaper and television advertising. And for the filmmakers and studio, it paid off, as *RoboCop* became a blockbuster (the sixteenth biggest hit of 1987), which means the film crossed over into acceptance by the general audience, and that it has been embraced by a fan base that has gone back for repeat viewings in theaters. (And you can bet that more than a few young teens were sneaking in to see it.)

This kind of success invariably means that a sequel is inevitable, and *RoboCop 2* arrived in 1990. But the second film was a critical and box-office disappointment, though it did manage to become moderately successful in terms of profit. So when it came time for *RoboCop 3*, it was decided to go for a PG-13 in hopes of reaching a wider audience. But the third time was not the charm and *RoboCop 3* was a critical and box-office flop. In terms of the rating, they got what they wanted, a label allowing teenagers to attend, despite the film's distinctly "adult" material—plenty of people being blown away, including innocent bystanders, although the camera cuts away more quickly and the spray of bullets is relatively bloodless. (There followed two watered-down, short-lived live-action *RoboCop* TV series and an equally short-lived pair of animated series. A 2013 remake of the original *RoboCop* returned the series to an R-rated level of violence and language.)

Despite their violence, with huge body counts, the generally bloodless *Star Wars* movies always managed to get by with a PG, until the last one. *Star Wars* (1977), *The Empire Strikes Back* (1980), and *Return of the Jedi* (1983) came out before the PG-13 was created, but in the late 1990s for George Lucas' re-edited versions, all three were still rated PG, this time with explanations.

The original *Star Wars* was rated PG for "sci-fi violence and brief mild language." *The Empire Strikes Back* and *Return of the Jedi* both earned PGs for "sci-fi action violence."

When Lucas came up with his prequel trilogy, *Star Wars: Episode I: The Phantom Menace* (1999) received a PG for "sci-fi action/violence" and *Star Wars: Episode II: Attack of the Clones* (2002) earned a PG for "sustained sequences of sci-fi action/violence." But the third, *Star Wars: Episode III: The Revenge of the Sith* (2005), became the first *Star Wars* movie to earn a PG-13, for "sci-fi violence and some intense images."

More intense than the very dark *The Empire Strikes Back*? Apparently so, at least in the minds of rating board members.

In the 1970s and '80s, people who attended PG-rated pictures were occasionally surprised to see nudity in movies where such a moment was completely unexpected, but it became less common in the 1990s—with one major exception, James Cameron's *Titanic* (1997). This film was rated PG-13 and became one of the biggest moneymaking movies of all time.

And although it obviously didn't hurt the film's success, there was quite a backlash during the film's initial release over a pair of scenes that occur during the soap-opera stories developed during *Titanic*'s first two hours, prior to the ship finally hitting the iceberg.

The film's central focus is on a pair of star-crossed lovers, a 17-year-old girl of privilege named Rose (Kate Winslet) and an impoverished, free-spirited artist called Jack (Leonardo DiCaprio). At one point Rose asks Jack to draw a nude portrait of her. She excuses herself for a moment, returns in a sheer nightgown, which she then drops to the ground, leaving little to the imagination, before reclining on a couch as Jack draws on a sketchpad. Later, there is also a steamy sexual encounter in an automobile onboard the ship.

In 2012, when *Titanic* received a 3D theatrical reissue before its Blu-ray debut in September, the nude scene was never even mentioned.

Again, in R-rated movies you get what you get. But in PG and PG-13 movies, this kind of thing is quite often a surprise, and especially so in a film that will be seen by youngsters and teenagers over and over again on home video, as was (and is) the case with *Titanic*.

Adam Sandler initially gained stardom on *Saturday Night Live*, and after supporting performances as an actor-for-hire in a few movies, he wrote and starred in *Billy Madison* (1995), marking his first official "Adam Sandler movie." It was a sort of a warning shot to parents, the kind of movie that was to come from him with regularity thereafter, each with elements to attract young teens and repel their parents, mainly far too much vulgarity and sexual material for its PG-13 rating.

In between his own films, Sandler has dabbled in offering more dramatic performances with the R-rated dramas *Punch-Drunk Love* (2002), *Reign Over Me* (2007) and *Funny People* (2009). And in 2012 he finally tackled a full-blown sleazy R-rated farce, *That's My Boy*, which is on par with the trashiest fare in that rating category, from *Knocked Up* (2007) to *The Hangover* (2009).

But Sandler's PG-13 movies are also awfully raunchy, some more than others, but none are really the kind of fare children should be viewing. Even when children play principle characters, as in *Billy Madison*, in which Sandler returns to grade school and is surrounded by kids, or *Big Daddy*, with Sandler being unexpectedly saddled with a five-year-old boy, complete with poster art depicting a scene from the film in which Sandler and the boy are urinating on the back doors of a posh restaurant.

Although I'm on the record as not being a fan of Sandler's films, I am also not oblivious to his talent. He can be charming and funny, and before he began writing and starring in his own pictures, he often stole the show from more seasoned veterans. In 1994, I singled him out for providing "big laughs" in the otherwise weak ensemble comedies *Airheads* and *Mixed Nuts*. He also played an amusing recurring character in four episodes of Bill Cosby's seminal sitcom *The Cosby Show*.

But Sandler's penchant for the puerile, in particular scatological and sexual gags, tends to undermine everything he does. It's a bit surprising to revisit something like the PG-13 rated *The Wedding Singer* (1998) and find that even his early work and one of his better films is so hindered by the frequent poor-taste joke.

Arguably, the most egregious example is his 2007 farce *You Don't Mess With the Zohan.* The film has Sandler playing his usual lovable doofus, but in this case with what is supposed to be a Middle Eastern accent. He stars as the title character, a superspy for the Israeli Mossad secret service who secretly harbors a desire to cut and style women's

Adam Sandler in You Don't Mess with the Zohan *(2008) —Columbia*

hair. So, while on a mission, he fakes his death and heads for New York, adopts the pseudonym "Scrappy Coco" and finds work in a salon owned by a beautiful Palestinian. There his penchant for retro cuts becomes a sensation, while jokes abound about "Zohan's" sexual prowess, which he at first just talks about, but then demonstrates with the customers whose hair he styles, mostly middle-aged to elderly women.

As a result, *Zohan* plays as the poster child for PG-13 movies that should be rated R.

Another *Saturday Night Live* veteran, Mike Myers, parlayed one of his characters from that show into movie stardom with *Wayne's World*, a hugely popular comedy about a pair of pop culture-spouting slackers, Wayne (Myers) and Garth (Dana Carvey), and their local cable-access television program. The film was number eight in the top-ten biggest moneymakers of 1992 and spawned a sequel the next year, *Wayne's World II*. Both were rather vulgar and sexual for their PG-13 ratings, but they were like Disney cartoons compared to what Myers came up with a few years later.

In 1997, Myers adopted a 1960s superspy persona for the James Bond spoof *Austin Powers: International Man of Mystery*, in which his title character is cryogenically frozen in 1967 and thawed out thirty years later. Naturally, his free-spirited nature clashes wildly with the political correctness of the '90s. Myers also plays Powers' nemesis, the villainous Dr. Evil. And the film earned a PG-13 rating, though it plays like an obvious candidate for an R.

Aimed directly at teenagers—despite the fact that it lampoons the excesses of the 1960s, an era long before they were born—the film was written and co-produced by Myers and it goes much, much further than *Wayne's World* in the raunch department. A vast majority of the gags have to do with sex or bodily functions, something often referred to by filmmakers and film critics as "adult" humor, despite the fact that it's really quite juvenile. And it hardly seems suitable for kids from thirteen to seventeen. Here are some examples:

★ All through the picture, Myers is trying to get women into bed, constantly dropping broad, vulgar sexual hints.

★ After he is thawed, Myers uses a urinal in a scene that goes on forever because, well, he's been asleep for thirty years.

★ In a public restroom, while Myers and Tom Arnold are sitting in adjoining stalls, Myers is attacked by an assassin and Arnold reacts to the noises being made, thinking they are . . . um . . . natural.

★ Fabiana Udenio plays an Italian bimbo/assassin (with huge breasts and cleavage down to there) whose character name is so vulgar I'm uncomfortable repeating it here but, suffice it to say, it's a variation on the equally vulgar name of Honor Blackman's character in *Goldfinger*.

★ In one scene, Udenio is in a hot tub, and Myers undresses to climb in with her . . . you can guess the rest.

★ At the end of the film, a nude Myers and Elizabeth Hurley walk around an apartment holding up various objects in carefully placed obscene positions to block (and mock) their private parts. The scene is capped by Hurley blowing up a long balloon in front of Myers' profile.

So, if I understand this correctly, all of these things are perfectly suitable for young teenagers, according to the rating board. And board members consider the use of the f-word on the soundtrack to describe certain acts as being much worse than the acts themselves being graphically and repeatedly portrayed on the screen.

The punchline here is that *Austin Powers: International Man of Mystery* was a very successful film, and the two sequels that followed, *Austin Powers: The Spy Who Shagged Me* (1999) and *Austin Powers in Goldmember* (2002), were even more successful, both landing in the top ten of their respective years' box-office records. And each was sleazier than the one before, yet still managed to hang on to those coveted PG-13 ratings. As you might guess, *Austin Powers 4* is in the works.

The battles over ratings are ongoing, and arguments over violence are not all that different than they were some forty years ago, except that the level of Grand Guignol gore has escalated—especially in R-rated movies. But it can be pretty gruesome in PG-13s, too. Take the 2011 thriller *Hanna* for example. I can honestly say I've never seen a PG-13 movie more deserving of an R for violence.

The lead character, whose name is Hanna (Saoirse Ronan), is a young teenage girl trained as an assassin, and the bodies of ruthless villains are not the only targets of our young killer to pile up in this film. Innocent, even compassionate, characters also bite the dust without anyone even suggesting a hint of regret. I don't care how much editing was done to *Hanna* to get the movie-rating committee to see it as a PG-13, it should have received an R. In fact, the filmmakers should have been told, "Sorry guys, this is an R-rated movie and nothing will make it acceptable for children's viewing."

Setting aside the graphic violence, what about the film's attitude? The first victim of our young executioner is someone sent to her as a decoy, a seemingly innocent woman who shows compassion and concern for Hanna, just before the girl slits her throat. True, she thinks at first that she has killed a villain, but later in the film, after Hanna discovers she instead killed someone who genuinely tried to reach out to her, it doesn't even seem to register. Toward the end of the picture, after a kind, sympathetic family has taken her in—a mother, father and two children—each member is tortured (off-camera, thankfully) and it is implied that all four are killed. But it's just a matter-of-fact element of the plot. No sorrow. No grief. No discussion. On to the inevitable one-on-one showdown between our heroine and the film's chief villain.

Why did the filmmakers even want a PG-13? Clearly, this level of remorseless mayhem is adult material. But the cynic in me says it's because a teenage assassin would be appealing to the teen audience.

Every so often a PG-13 animated feature comes along that seems to pose the question, who is this for? It's too raunchy for children, too silly for adults and even teenagers tend to shun such films.

There are also occasional R-rated animated features, but they are pitched to adults, tout the rating, and that's usually enough to tell you where they're coming from—*Heavy Metal* (1981), *American Pop* (1981), *Hey Good Lookin'* (1982), *South Park: Bigger, Longer & Uncut* (1999), *Waking Life* (2001).

The PG-13s, however, are usually sold directly to young children, despite a rating that suggests they shouldn't be. One example is *Adam Sandler's Eight Crazy Nights* (2002), a musical cartoon comedy set against Hanukkah, with the main character being an alcoholic ex-con sentenced to community service with a youth basketball league, a film replete with crude language, sleazy sex gags, vulgar dialogue, and tasteless humor.

Another, *Cool World* (1992), has a cartoonist discovering his drawings are linked to a real animated world, and when he has sex with a cartoon character she becomes human.

Bebe's Kids (1992) is much more tame by comparison, the story of a single man saddled with rowdy kids at an amusement park, but it does have some foul language and vulgar gags.

Ditto *The Simpsons Movie* (2007), which is just about what you might expect from this TV show spinoff.

In January 2004, a romantic comedy called *Win a Date With Tad Hamilton!* opened— a slight slice of fluff that plays like a throwback to another era, when movies about teens and twenty-somethings were cheery and innocent, and there were no real bad guys. It's not hard to envision this picture with a cast from the early 1960s: Sandra Dee in the Kate Bosworth role of the small-town girl who enters a contest to win a date with a movie star; Jim Hutton in the Topher Grace role, as the boy who has known her since they were children and loves her from afar; George Hamilton in the Josh Duhamel role as the movie star; Connie Francis in the Ginnifer Goodwin role as the comical, plain-Jane best girlfriend; James Stewart in the Gary Cole role as Bosworth's father, pretending to be hip to the ways of Hollywood (think *Take Her, She's Mine*).

Win a Date With Tad Hamilton! is no groundbreaking or star-making film—and just this once I'll set aside my prejudice against movies that have exclamation points in their titles! But it is a nice, amusing, pleasant picture with virtually nothing offensive. So why is it rated PG-13? Here's a film where none of the characters have sex (except the movie star, off-screen and implied). In fact, Kate Bosworth's lead character *declines* to have sex with the movie star. When's the last time something like that happened in a major-studio film? And there is very little vulgar or profane language, and no violence.

Putting this into context for 2004, *Tad Hamilton* seemed to me to be so clean that a PG rating should have been assured. And yet it has the same PG-13 rating as these films that were playing in theaters when *Tad Hamilton* opened:

★ *Chasing Liberty*, a Mandy Moore comedy with her character, the U.S. president's daughter, eluding Secret Service agents to, essentially, go out and lose her virginity, which she ultimately does. The film also has offensive language and some nudity.

★ *In America*, a dramatic look at an illegal-immigrant family from Ireland trying to eke out a living in Manhattan, with a fairly graphic sex scene with nudity, along with quite a bit of language—including the f-word—and some violence.

- ★ *Intolerable Cruelty*, a dark comedy by the Coen Brothers starring George Clooney and Catherine Zeta-Jones, with a goodly amount of profanity—f-word included—some sexual discussion and activity, and nude photos.
- ★ *Something's Gotta Give*, a romantic comedy starring Diane Keaton and Jack Nicholson, with profanity—including the f-word—sexual talk and activity, and nudity.
- ★ *Stuck on You*, a broad farce by the Farrelly Brothers, featuring Matt Damon and Greg Kinnear as conjoined twins, with extremely crude language—including the f-word—along with sexual references and activity, and violence.
- ★ *Torque*, a chase thriller with Ice Cube as a biker, which contains a lot of violence, some profanity—including the f-word—and many scantily clad women, with their body parts frequently shown in close-up shots.
- ★ *Under the Tuscan Sun*, a romantic melodrama with Diane Lane as a writer on vacation in Tuscany who buys a villa on a whim; a film that has sex, partial nudity, and profanity—including, as if you couldn't guess by now, the f-word.

Note that all of these movies are also clearly "adult" in their themes and storylines, and that they are obviously geared toward the eighteen and older crowd. So, again, why are they rated PG-13, which implies they are fine for thirteen-year-olds, albeit with parental discretion?

This is, of course, the way of the world, which came crashing home to me one weekend in 2004. My wife and I turned off a video and found the television was on the local ABC affiliate, which was airing Jim Carrey's 1997 comedy *Liar Liar* in a 6 p.m. time slot. As the film broke for commercials, it turned out it was being shown on, of all programs, *The Wonderful World of Disney*. True, the very raunchy *Liar Liar* was edited, but not nearly enough.

The preview of the next week's movie on this Disney program was for *A Bug's Life*. Obviously, putting the extremely sexual *Liar Liar* on the same level as a Pixar animated family film is just too ridiculous. Carrey fans might argue that *Liar Liar* is about a boy who wishes his lawyer-father into telling the truth for one day, and that there's a happy-family ending . . . but for a film replete with inappropriate sexual scenes and dialogue, by the time that happy ending arrives it's too little too late.

And, of course, *Liar Liar* —in its unedited form—is rated PG-13. And when it was in production, I'm guessing the filmmakers never intended for it to be a children's film that would be shown on an early-evening Disney program.

Christopher Nolan's trilogy of *Batman* movies kicked off in 2005 with *Batman Begins*, a dark, violent, revisionist look at the comic-book hero, starring Christian Bale. But there really wasn't any special controversy over the film's PG-13, which was, after all, on par with Tim Burton's two *Batman* movies of the 1980s. Then, in 2008, we got Nolan's second film in the franchise, *The Dark Knight*, and that one really caused a stir because it was so very dark and angry and mean-spirited, with a chief villain—Heath Ledger's Oscar-winning turn as the Joker—that many found quite disturbing. And yet it too earned a PG-13 rating. There were a lot of complaints at the time, but fast-forward to summer 2012 and the equally dark *The Dark Knight Rises* also carries a PG-13 with virtually no discussion, much less expressions of outrage.

Turning the *Batman* comics into movies always seems to court controversy. Parental concerns also swirled around the second of Tim Burton's two *Batman* films. The first Burton-directed *Batman* in 1989 had its share of critics with reference to its rating, due to the film being sold to children despite being very dark and violent. But the 1992 sequel was much darker and this time carried a grotesque, mean-spirited attitude that made it even more troubling for kids, yet this one was also sold directly to them. If *Indiana Jones and the Temple of Doom* was too much for the PG rating, many parents were concerned that

Batman Returns was too much for the PG-13.

When I reviewed *Batman Returns*, I wrote that it was "darker, more brooding and weirder than the first," and that in some ways "it falls prey to its own excesses. The violence is quite gruesome in places and there are far too many vulgar, sex-related gags for a movie aimed primarily at young people." I cited as reasons for the rating, based on my own interpretation of the material, "quite a bit of violence and mayhem, too many vulgar jokes, and a few profanities."

A surprising number of other 1992 films also seemed to raise the hackles of parents, led by *Death Becomes Her*, a dark absurdist fantasy about two aging women (Meryl Streep and Goldie Hawn) at war with each other, using magical powers to keep themselves from aging and ultimately destroying each other's bodies in a manner that resembles Bugs Bunny's battles with Daffy Duck. My review described the content this way: "It is rated PG-13, which seems awfully tame considering the amount of violence involved, not to mention the surprising amount of gratuitous female nudity."

Other PG-13 movies that year that had parents up in arms included *Prelude to a Kiss* and *The Playboys*, a pair of adult romantic comedies that show the lead characters in sexual situations; *City of Joy*, a film with some incredibly disturbing and stark scenes of violence; *Ladybugs* and *Radio Flyer*, two movies aimed directly at children, the first a vulgar comedy that has jokes that imply child sexual abuse and the second a fantasy that trivializes violent child abuse; and *This Is My Life*, an adult comedy that features a comic scene where a young teenage girl and boy attempt to have sex, with the main joke involving the boy struggling with a condom.

How are movies like this really appropriate for young minds?

In June 1997, my oldest daughter Jennifer called me with a movie question. She already knew what I'd say, but that's OK since she was actually looking more for confirmation than an answer. It seemed that my grandson Connor, five years old at the time, had been nagging her about seeing a new superhero movie, the fourth in the *Batman* franchise that was started by Tim Burton. The film was *Batman & Robin*, starring George Clooney as the masked avenger. "Is that something I should let him see?" Jennifer asked. "I haven't let him see the other *Batman* movies. But is this one less violent or something?"

It seems that a slight doubt entered her mind about this particular *Batman* picture because of the flood of advertising and merchandising aimed directly at Connor's age group. Ads for *Batman & Robin* had been airing during the TV cartoon shows that Connor sometimes watched in the afternoon—*Bobby's World*, *Spider-Man* and, of course, *Batman & Robin*. The *Batman* cartoon was a particular selling point for the movie since both carried the same title.

George Clooney and Chris O'Donnell in Joel Schumacher's Batman & Robin *(1997) —Warner Bros.*

If that wasn't enough, when Jennifer's family went to Taco Bell the previous week, Connor saw Batman posters on the walls and windows, Batman mobiles hanging from the ceiling, a Batman toy in the kids meal . . . it was Batman Land with Mexican food (if you can call what they serve at Taco Bell "Mexican food"). As a result, before *Batman & Robin* opened, the film was on the mind of many a young child, as well as teens and adults. No wonder it took in nearly $44 million in its first three days (and that was 1997 dollars).

As Jennifer put it at the time, this is the mass-media equivalent of twisting children's arms so that they will twist their parents' arms. "Connor came up to me and said, 'Mom! The Batman movie starts Friday!' And I said, 'Now, Connor, we haven't let you see the others, so we probably won't let you see this one, either.' You know, five-year-olds are so into superheroes—but they don't make superhero movies they can go see."

Oh, you can argue that Hollywood gave us the Power Rangers movie *Turbo* a few months before this, and then *Warriors of Virtue*, about martial-arts kangaroos (I'm not kidding), both of which were rated PG. But Jennifer judged the latter to be too violent (she was right) and though she succumbed to *Turbo*, it turned out that Connor didn't like it. "He said it was lame," Jennifer said.

And maybe that's the problem. Hollywood is having such a difficult time coming up with films that are appropriate for children that it's taken to selling them films that are wildly inappropriate. *Batman & Robin* was merely the most recent example in 1997.

The modern equivalent would be the *Transformers* trilogy, a summer-movie franchise that kicked off in 2007, with sequels released in 2009 and 2011. The first movie set the tone for those to follow, with noisy, chaotic action and massive destruction (courtesy of computer animation) in a story about a warring race of robots that can transform into everyday mechanical objects, and how one side recruits a nerdy teen (Shia LaBeouf) to help save the world.

The filmmakers might argue that *Transformers* is intended for teenagers and older action fans—but it's based on a children's toy, and all three films were blatantly sold to children by marketing toys and other merchandise, along with TV ads for Pepsi, and posters, banners, etc., adorning Burger King restaurants. Of course, the fact that the first film earned $300 million and was the No. 3 movie of 2007 indicates that the audience that embraced it went beyond just children. But the fact remains that it is an awfully attractive concept for youngsters, and the marketers made no bones about pursuing and exploiting that young audience.

The violence and chaos of the *Transformers* trilogy is bad enough, but there's another aspect that seems wildly inappropriate for pictures like these, and that's the in-your-face sexuality on display. There are comically inappropriate sexual discussions between LaBeouf's character and his parents, plus the camera repeatedly ogling in close-ups of the scantily clad body of Megan Fox in the first two and Rosie Huntington-Whiteley in the third.

Allowing movies like this to carry PG-13 ratings seems way off the mark. Although, since the second two *Transformers* films were also huge box-office hits, I have to wonder if the parents of the kids that made these movies so successful were aware of the films' content, aside from the heavily advertised robot action.

Personally, I find the gradual evolution of PG-13 movies from teen to adult fare quite distressing—how can movies that are deemed suitable for young teens contain so much sexual material when they shouldn't have any at all? To me it confirms that the people who rate the movies—and especially the people who make the movies— have officially lost their minds.

Sexual content has become so commonplace in PG-13 pictures that many of us who attend movies regularly have become numb to it. Not a good thing.

But every now and then, something comes along that shocks even seasoned, jaded filmgoers. In 2008, it was a scene in the Christmas comedy *Yes Man*, starring Jim Carrey as a down-in-the-dumps fellow who is coerced into saying yes to anything and everything for one year. Much of the film is vulgar, but the shocker is a moment when an elderly woman performs a sexual act as the camera goes to Carrey's gyrating face. It isn't funny. It isn't pretty. And it definitely isn't something kids should see. And what is a movie like this doing with a PG-13 rating?

And yet, there it is. Oral sex is implied, but never explicit in quite a few PG and PG-13 films, usually with the camera traveling up to the gyrating face of the male recipient, often for comic effect. And it's been around ever since *Airplane!* (1980), in which Julie Hagerty blows into an air valve located in the crotch of a life-size, uniformed blow-up doll that is deflating. The doll is the plane's "automatic pilot," nicknamed "Otto," and when it is fully inflated, the painted expression changes from emotionless to a smile.

In *Ghostbusters* (1984), a ghost unzips Dan Aykroyd's pants and he makes a goofy face. In *Ace Ventura, Pet Detective* (1994), it is implied that this is the way a client intends to "pay" for Jim Carrey's services. And so it goes, all the way up to *Dark Shadows* (2012), with a psychiatrist (Helena Bonham Carter) attempting to uniquely earn the trust of a vampire (Johnny Depp).

Just as adult and extremely kid-unfriendly are the PG and PG-13 films *3 Men and a Baby* (1987) and its sequel, *Waterworld* (1995), *My Best Friend's Wedding* (1997), *The Fifth Element* (1997), *Bring it On* (2000), *Meet the Parents* (2000) and its sequels, *Charlie's Angels* (2000) and its sequel, *The Fast and the Furious* (2001) and its sequels, *Pearl Harbor* (2001), *Mr. & Mrs. Smith* (2005), *Memoirs of a Geisha* (2005), *Taken* (2008) and its sequel, *The Time Traveler's Wife* (2009), *The Lovely Bones* (2009), *17 Again* (2009), *Burlesque* (2010), *Salt* (2010), *The Switch* (2010), *Limitless* (2011), *Larry Crowne* (2011) and many more.

Then, there is the adult comedy *Salmon Fishing in the Yemen* (2012), which is largely benign, although it has a subplot about an unhappily married man falling in love with another woman, and a sex scene between a husband and wife that is brief and under the covers, but nonetheless, explicit and inappropriate for the PG-13 rating.

Other 2012 PG-13 movies that were either sex-laced or had sexual moments that felt as if they should have been out of bounds for their PG-13 ratings included *The Lucky One*, *Think Like a Man*, *Girl in Progress*, *What to Expect When You're Expecting*, *Rock of Ages*, *People Like Us*, *Hope Springs*, *Total Recall*, etc.

Historically, most publicized fights with the rating board have involved films that received an X or NC-17 but wanted the more distribution-friendly R. But in the 21st century there's been a shift, so that filmmakers these days more often have received an R but seek a PG-13—and they usually get it without trimming much, if anything.

Most R- and PG-13-rated movies have potentially offensive content in order to achieve what filmmakers refer to as "realism" or to make it more "adult." Which is, of course, a fallacy. Movies are, by their very nature, never "realistic." They are projected images on a larger-than-life screen, and though some reflect real-life situations, challenges, or relationships better than others, they remain illusions.

How does extremely gory violence, or characters spouting foul language, or displays of graphic sex and nudity, or tasteless gags and childish behavior make a movie more adult? So much offensive content is so obviously gratuitous that it could easily be omitted with absolutely no affect whatsoever on the integrity of the movie. In the end, if the movie is good, it shouldn't matter what the rating is.

Everyone knows that when kids turn thirteen they feel they've reached a moviegoing watermark and should be able to see any PG-13 movie that comes along. They see this as something akin to turning sixteen and being able to drive or turning eighteen and being able to vote. So, along comes Hollywood, tempting thirteen-year-olds with plenty of violent or vulgar PG-13-rated movies, accompanied by TV and online ad campaigns aimed at youngsters, sometimes a lot younger than thirteen.

According to the Webster's dictionary on my desk—yes, I still sometimes look up words in a hardbound book instead of using the array of online dictionaries—there are many definitions of "family," but this is the one that applies to "family movies": "designed or suitable for both children and adults." So maybe it's the definition of "suitable" that seems to elude so many filmmakers and television producers in Hollywood.

There is no censorship in the movies these days, except for whatever the filmmaker himself might decree, but the Motion Picture Association of America would be doing parents a greater service if it cracked down on movies with this kind of content. An R-rating would better protect the children and warn the parents. Of course, the PG-13 rating has never really been what the label implies. The PG means "parental guidance" and the thirteen means if your kid is a teenager—thirteen to seventeen—this movie's just hunky-dory; or at least that's how most people interpret it.

Unfortunately, the movie industry has painted itself into a corner because if these movies did receive R ratings, they might not be as successful as they are with PG-13s. True, extremely hard R-rated movies like *Bridesmaids*, the two *Hangover* films and *Ted*, among others, have been big hits, but they are anomalies. In general, that rating tends to chase a portion of the audience away. And that's the real reason these lighter, softer films don't get R ratings for what is clearly adult material.

And it's why such very violent PG-13 movies as *Hanna* or the *Taken* revenge flicks (2008/2012) or the remake of *Red Dawn* (2012), and such sexualized films as *Crazy, Stupid, Love* or *Rock of Ages* or *Hope Springs* and others have made me wonder if the rating board didn't go in the wrong direction when it came up with PG-13 in 1984.

Instead of a variation on PG, maybe it should have been a variation on R—R-lite, perhaps. Or split the R down the middle; R-soft and R-hard. Something closer to Steven Spielberg's flippant (or maybe not so flippant) suggestion of R-12, only bumped up to R-16 or R-18, so that high schoolers won't be exposed to the violence, sex, and obscene language so many PG-13 movies contain these days.

Chapter 5

THE PG RATING

An Endangered Species

For the first decade-and-a-half the PG (M/GP) rating was the catch-all filter. No one wanted an X because, in general, it pared down the audience considerably, bringing in fewer ticket buyers than any other rating. This was especially true after the first year or two of CARA's existence, when the X came to be thought of as the rating for "dirty" movies. And that was an understandable public perception since, ultimately, the X—the only rating that was not trademarked by the MPAA—was co-opted by the pornographic-movie industry.

On the other end of the spectrum, no one wanted a G because films with that rating were thought to be for children. Never mind that adult movies often came away with G ratings in the early days; it didn't take long before the rating somehow became equated with cartoons aimed at small fry.

Thus, the PG became the go-to rating of choice for most mainstream movies that wanted to reach a wider audience than the more adult R rating allowed.

All that changed when the PG-13 came into existence. From mid-1984 on, the PG rating was gradually used less and less until it finally became just one small step up from G. The thinking today seems to be that if the PG-13 is for anyone from young teens to adults, and the G is for toddlers, then the PG must be for "tweens," youngsters who are not quite teenagers but no longer young children, the way-station for passing time until they reach age 13, because that's when the doors open to the good stuff, the previously forbidden fruit of the PG-13 that their older siblings and parents get to watch.

The 2011 films *Prom* and *Monte Carlo* are examples of movies for tweens, films that would be right at home on the Disney Channel, sandwiched between *Good Luck Charlie* and *Austin & Ally*. (Literally, since *Prom* is a Disney movie.) And if you read the reviews for *Prom* and *Monte Carlo* you may see the phrase "old-fashioned" used repeatedly, as if anything remotely clean, wholesome, and uplifting must hark back to another, earlier era. And such efforts are, unfortunately, the rare exception. More often, movies about teenagers involve underage indiscretions, such as drinking alcohol, sexual activity, vulgar dialogue, and sometimes the use of drugs, ranging from marijuana smoking to cocaine snorting to the misuse of prescription drugs.

But that doesn't mean modern PG movies are bereft of inappropriate material. The 2001 animated fairy tale spoof *Shrek*, which has (so far) spawned several short cartoons and three feature-length sequels—*Shrek 2* (2004), *Shrek the Third* (2007), and *Shrek Forever After* (2010)—is never far from a crude, vulgar gag that would be more at home in a raunchy teen comedy. Each of the *Shrek* features has been rated PG, for "crude humor," "rude humor," "suggestive content," etc., and the tasteless jokes usually involve innuendo before a quick cutaway. Most of these jokes are subtle enough to fly over the head of the average child—but as the films are watched over and over again by children and teens, these gags are drummed into their impressionable little minds. In other words, this kind of material seems way out of line for movies aimed at kids.

Then there's *Marley & Me* (2008), which from its advertising appeared to be very much a family-friendly film about a Florida couple

(Owen Wilson, Jennifer Aniston), two newspaper writers, who raise a rambunctious Labrador retriever puppy along with their children. A true story based on the memoir by John Grogan, the film actually is quite charming much of the way, but it also includes foul language, sexual innuendo, and veiled nudity, which takes it out of the family-friendly realm and points toward, at least, a PG-13 rating.

All of this is, of course both sad and ridiculous. The idea that a clean movie must be dirtied up a bit in order to attract an older audience is a slap in the face to intelligent, thoughtful adults—and their children—who go to movies to be entertained, not insulted. Throwing in a few naughty words or something vulgar or disgusting just to keep a movie from getting a G or PG rating is actually an indication that the filmmakers either have contempt for moviegoers or don't have much confidence in their own work. If it's a good movie it will in all likelihood find its audience. For all the reliance by movie studios on statistical charts and graphs, and on polls and focus groups, word-of-mouth is still the best way for a movie to rise to the top.

From 1968 to 1984, PG movies included some distinctly adult fare. Earlier chapters have noted such films as Steven Spielberg's *Indiana Jones and the Temple of Doom*, *Gremlins* and *Poltergeist* as examples of movies that were considered too harsh for PGs, but not quite harsh enough for Rs, and, therefore, led directly to the creation of the PG-13 rating. But a lot of other distinctly adult movies with questionable content were also rated PG during those years before the PG-13 came along.

A well-known and still popular example is the Oscar-winning and very influential dark satirical comedy *The Graduate*, with Dustin Hoffman as laconic college grad Benjamin Braddock and Anne Bancroft as Mrs. Robinson, the seductive neighbor who is twice his age, which came out in 1967, two years before the ratings were installed. Then, in 1972, the film was rated PG for a theatrical reissue. *The Graduate* is built around the theme of adultery and the impact it has on two families that have been friendly for years. In terms of content, it contains scattered profanities, flashes of nudity during the initial seduction sequence, a startling moment with a stripper in a nightclub, and many instances of sexual contact. An obvious candidate for an R rating, the surprise PG raised a lot of eyebrows in 1972.

To see sexuality and nudity in PG movies from the 1970s and '80s is not that uncommon, although CARA at the time claimed to keep them separate. Sexual material was allowed if it was alluded to or wasn't graphic or specific, and nudity was allowed if it was non-sexual, such as a shower scene or a sequence in a gym or locker room, or someone at home dressing or undressing, etc.

Of course, sexuality is in the eye of the beholder. In *Transformers,* for example, when a young woman in tight shorts and a revealing top is leaning over a car to inspect the engine, and the camera goes up and down her torso, forcing the audience to ogle her, is that sexual? It would seem a deliberate choice by the director to indeed sexualize a teenage girl (played by Megan Fox, who was actually in her early twenties at the time)—and in a movie based on a toy and aimed directly at young people.

Movie critics love the word "gratuitous" and it is frequently used when violence or sex or foul language or drug use or nudity are displayed for reasons that appear to have little or nothing at all to do with the story or action on the screen. To my way of thinking, really gory violence, graphic sexuality, redundant foul language, and nudity are almost always gratuitous.

Motion pictures are such a literal medium—on a huge screen in a darkened auditorium with cranked-up stereo sound so that the focus of the audience is strictly on the film—that a little subtlety would seem to be called for. When an actor puts something across with just a look—a raised eyebrow, pursed lips, or an expressive facial gesture blown up to an oversized, unrealistic dimension—it doesn't take much to convey a feeling or thought. So, by its very nature, everything in a movie is exaggerated. Why compound that by hitting the audience over the head when a hint would be more than enough?

In live theater the actors are taught to play big and loud for the benefit of patrons on the back row. In a movie theater, even the back row feels like the front row, and playing big and loud or explicit and graphic is simply overkill, and often has the effect of undermining the writer or director's original intent, making it feel too broad and over-the-top.

Once nudity began to be allowed in mainstream American movies during the late 1960s and into the '70s, filmmakers seemed to be actively looking for reasons to have actors doff their clothing, and that included PG films, though the nudity was, according to CARA rules, supposed to be non-sexual. It was almost exclusively women taking off their clothes and it was often so gratuitous that it seemed to come out of nowhere, taking audience members aback. Examples include the PG-rated *Romeo and Juliet* (1968), *Ryan's Daughter* (which carried a GP until 1996 when it was re-rated for home video and received an R), *Barry Lyndon* (1975), *Coma* (1978), *Invasion of the Body Snatchers* (1978), *Hair* (1979), *Can't Stop the Music* (1980), *Tribute* (1980), *How to Beat the High Co$t of Living* (1980), *Ragtime* (1981), *Looker* (1981), *I Ought to Be in Pictures* (1982), *The Beastmaster* (1982), *Irreconcilable Differences* (1984), *Sheena* (1984), and many more.

This trend was interrupted in 1984 when the PG-13 took over, and within a few years more and more sexual content began to creep into movies with that rating—so that now audiences need to be as wary of PG-13 movies as they are of Rs.

One of the earliest films that should probably have been rated R for sex, but walked away with a PG, is *Barbarella* (1968), a sexualized outer-space fantasy based on a French comic strip, starring Jane Fonda during her sexpot era when she was married to French filmmaker and provocateur Roger Vadim, the director of this picture. There is quite a bit of sexual content and nudity, though the latter is mostly veiled in various ways. The film carried no rating when it was released in October 1968, but earned a PG when it was rated for a 1977 re-release.

Foul language in PG films was usually scattered, but once in awhile a movie would come along that seemed to push things, and not necessarily with the f-word. A now largely forgotten film called

The Idolmaker (1980), about a songwriter (Ray Sharkey) who grooms and promotes Elvis Presley-style singers as teen idols, had a steady stream of foul language using every word you can think of (and some you can't)—except the f-word. And once a movie like that gets a PG rating, the gloves are off, and more PG-rated films begin to exhibit extreme language.

As for violence, need we say more than "Clint Eastwood"? After gaining some amount of stardom in the TV series *Rawhide*, Eastwood went to Spain and starred in three Italian-funded westerns, now referred to as the *Dollar Trilogy* or *The Man With No Name Trilogy—A Fistful of Dollars* (1964), *For a Few Dollars More* (1965) and *The Good, the Bad and the Ugly* (1966). All three were released in the United States for the first time in 1967, before the ratings were in place. In 1969, they were rated for re-releases and each received an M, the rating equivalent of what is now PG. But when the three films were re-submitted for home-video ratings in the late 1980s and early '90s, each received an R "for violence," which is what they now officially carry.

The trilogy made Eastwood's name and he returned home a worldwide superstar, ready for his first lead role in an American movie, *Hang 'Em High* (1968), a Hollywood picture directed in a style similar to his so-called "spaghetti westerns." A violent picture, *Hang 'Em High* was also rated M, the PG-equivalent at the time, for its initial release, then for home video in 1997 received a PG-13 "for western action violence."

Most of Eastwood's other pre-1984 movies are rated R, but he did make several PGs during this period, all of which are patently adult: *Where Eagles Dare* (1968), a World War II action tale co-starring Richard Burton, with plenty of violence and a few scattered profanities; *Two Mules for Sister Sara* (1970), a western with Shirley MacLaine as a nun (maybe), with quite a bit of violence and some implied sex; *Kelly's Heroes* (1970), a World War II comedy, with violence and a fair amount of profanity and vulgarity; *Joe Kidd* (1972), a western co-starring Robert Duvall, with violence and profanity; *Every Which Way But Loose* (1978) and *Any Which Way You Can* (1980), farcical redneck comedies with quite a lot of sex, nudity, profanity, vulgarity, and bare-knuckle violence; *Escape From Alcatraz* (1979), a prison-escape picture with violence, profanity, and nudity; *Bronco Billy* (1980), a comedy about a modern-day wild-west show, with sexual content, profanity, and violence; *Firefox* (1982), a Cold War thriller, with violence; *Honkytonk Man* (1982), a melodrama about a country singer on the skids, with sexuality and some language; and the period comedy *City Heat* (1984), with Eastwood and Burt Reynolds investigating a murder in the 1930s, with mild language, some sexuality, and an awful lot of violence.

Perhaps Eastwood's most surprising PG-rated film is *The Outlaw Josey Wales* (1976), a very violent post-Civil War revenge tale, with a great deal of graphic violence, rather explicit sex, and plenty of foul

Clint Eastwood directed and stars in The Outlaw Josey Wales *(1976) —Warner Bros.*

language, along with a particularly disturbing extended rape scene with nudity. One can only suppose that the rating-board members napped through this one.

Here are some other adult PG movies from the pre-PG-13 era:

★ *The Lion in Winter* (1968), the Oscar-winning adaptation of the play about King Henry II (Peter O'Toole) sparring with his wife, Eleanor of Aquitaine (Katharine Hepburn). Nothing offensive is shown, but there is a lot of gritty language and discussion, including repeated uses of Lord's name being taken in vain. Initially released unrated, the film earned a PG for a 1975 reissue.

★ *Butch Cassidy and the Sundance Kid* (1969), the famous western comedy starring Paul Newman and Robert Redford, was rated M for its first release, then was re-rated in 1974 for a reissue and earned the M equivalent, a PG. The film contains violence and foul language, and some sexual innuendo.

★ *And Now for Something Completely Different* (1971), an irreverent collection of comedy skits reworked from the popular British television series, *Monty Python's Flying Circus,* with violence, nudity, sex, and discussions about sex, all played for laughs. This was the Python sextet's first film and it received a GP rating, re-rated to PG the next year.

★ *The Born Losers* (1967) and *Billy Jack* (1971), low-budget, independent films that gained tremendous word-of-mouth popularity, each with an odd peace-through-violence message. They were the initial entries in a franchise by Tom Laughlin, who was both filmmaker and star. They also kicked off a popular cycle of taking-the-law-into-your-own-hands pictures during the 1970s, almost all of them rated R, the most popular being *Walking Tall* (1973) and *Death Wish* (1974), both of which also spawned sequels.

Despite the violence (including rape), nudity, and language (including the f-word) in some of the *Billy Jack* movies, the first three were rated PG or the equivalent. *Born Losers* went out unrated in 1967, but earned a PG for its 1974 reissue, and *Billy Jack* was rated GP when first released and was never re-rated. The third in the series, *The Trial of Billy Jack* (1974), was also rated PG. And the fourth, *Billy Jack Goes to Washington* (1977), was not released theatrically and has never been submitted for a rating, although it is widely available on DVD. (A fifth film has been in the works for many years, but has yet to materialize.)

★ *Young Frankenstein* (1974), Mel Brooks and Gene Wilder's wildly popular, oft-quoted spoof of old black-and-white *Frankenstein* films from the 1930s and '40s, is loaded with crass gags, sexual innuendo, and vulgarity.

★ The PG-rated *Jaws* (1975), one of the most popular movies of all time, is a scary ride for kids, and it contains quite a bit of bloody mayhem, a fair amount of profanity, some vulgar gags, and veiled nudity in the famous opening sequence. In 1975, filmmakers argued that *Jaws* should have a PG rating instead of an R, despite the bloody images on the screen, because it was animal-to-human violence, and, therefore could not be imitated by young viewers. The first two sequels, *Jaws 2* and *Jaws 3D* (1978/1983) are also rated PG, despite similar content. The last entry, *Jaws: The Revenge* was rated PG-13 in 1987.

★ *Grease* (1978) was an enormously popular musical comedy set in 1950s Southern California against the backdrop of Rydell High, focusing on the senior class and primarily the peer pressure that strains the relationship between Danny and Sandy, played by 24-year-old John Travolta and 30-year-old Olivia Newton-John. There is quite a bit of sexual material, including dialogue exchanges and some song lyrics, mostly spoofing 1950s attitudes, all of which raises eyebrows considering the young target audience for the film. That's especially true of the final sequence, when, in order to win her man, Sandy more or less abandons her virginal image and goes slutty, a dubious message if ever there was one.

★ *Being There* (1979) was Peter Sellers' penultimate film before his death, a comedy that won him an Oscar nomination as Chance, a simple-minded gardener who has never been outside a Washington, D.C., townhouse. In his middle age after his benefactor dies, he's rescued by a wealthy family and begins mingling with politicians who take his TV-inspired homilies as deep wisdom. There's a fair amount of foul language here, but one scene in particular is surprising in a PG-rated movie, as Shirley MacLaine's character, wearing a nightgown, but unable to seduce Chance, masturbates in front of him.

★ *Kramer vs. Kramer* (1979) is the multiple-Oscar-winning movie about a workaholic dad (Dustin Hoffman) who is abandoned by his wife (Meryl Streep) and left to raise their young son alone, which ultimately changes his priorities, especially his attitudes about fatherhood. Aside from scattered profanity, there is a sequence where a co-worker (Jobeth Williams) spends the night, and the next morning she is nude as she gets out of bed, goes down the hall, and bumps into the little boy. It's played for laughs, but not a lot is left to the imagination as the woman and the boy have a brief conversation.

★ *Airplane!* (1980) is a hugely popular lampoon of disaster pictures (and lots of other movies as well), which purloined the absurdist, off-the-wall comedy style of Mel Brooks' R-rated *Blazing Saddles* from five years earlier and applied it to a wider range of subject, sparking a popular movie-spoof trend that still occasionally crops up. *Airplane!* also included a great deal of sexual comedy, some extremely vulgar gags, and female nudity, all of which still seems to cry out for an R rating. Same goes for *Airplane II: The Sequel* (1982).

★ The Oscar-winning *Terms of Endearment* (1983), about a young wife/mother (Debra Winger), and her volatile relationship with her own mother (Shirley MacLaine), has sex talk, some sexual contact, and though there is not a lot of profanity, there are two usages of the f-word. This film sparked a lot of discussion about the rating system at the time after it initially received an R, but managed to have it overturned on appeal, so that the film went into theaters with a PG.

★ *Romancing the Stone* (1984) and *Jewel of the Nile* (1985) are romantic comedy-adventures that borrow quite a bit from the Indiana Jones films, with Michael Douglas as a reckless adventurer and Kathleen Turner as a romance writer. The first film's level of violence, profanity, and sexuality seems way out of sync with its PG rating, though the second film was softened a bit, with the exception of one usage of the f-word (despite this being after the PG-13 was in place).

★ Then, of course, there is the James Bond franchise, a fifty-year series of twenty-three movies that are all very violent and very sexual thrillers about British secret agent 007, licensed to kill. (There were also two movies made outside the official series before the PG-13 came into play, the 1967 spoof *Casino Royale* and *Never Say Never Again* in 1983.)

The earliest Bond pictures were made before there were ratings: *Dr. No* (1962), *From Russia With Love* (1963), *Goldfinger* (1964), *Thunderball* (1965), and *You Only Live Twice* (1967), all starring Sean Connery. Upon being reissued in the 1970s, each of these films received a PG rating or the equivalent. In 1970, *Thunderball* and *You Only Live Twice* were reissued with GP ratings, changed to PG for 1994 home-video releases. Similarly, for 1971 theatrical re-releases, *Dr. No, From Russia, With*

Sean Connery as James Bond visits Japan in You Only Live Twice *(1967) — United Artists*

Love, and *Goldfinger* earned GP ratings, which were also changed to PG in 1994. The next Bond movie was released in 1969, *On Her Majesty's Secret Service,* starring George Lazenby after Connery left the series. That film earned an M rating, which was changed to PG in 1994. Then came Connery's return to the role for *Diamonds Are Forever* (1971), rated GP, changed to PG in 1994.

Roger Moore took over the role next, and all of his films were rated PG from the get-go: *Live and Let Die* (1973), *The Man With the Golden Gun* (1974), *The Spy Who Loved Me* (1977), *Moonraker* (1979), *For Your Eyes Only* (1981), *Octopussy* (1983), and *A View to a Kill* (1985). (In 1983, Connery returned to the role for one more 007 adventure, a remake of *Thunderball* that was produced independently, outside of the official franchise, titled *Never Say Never Again*, also rated PG.)

Next up was Timothy Dalton, who starred in only two Bond films. The first, *The Living Daylights* (1987), earned a PG. The second, *Licence to Kill* (1989), became the first Bond movie to receive a PG-13 rating, and it set the pace for all that followed. The four starring Pierce Brosnan and the three (so far) starring Daniel Craig, have all received PG-13 ratings: *GoldenEye* (1995), *Tomorrow Never Dies* (1997), *The World Is Not Enough* (1999), *Die Another Day* (2002), *Casino Royale* (2006), *Quantum of Solace* (2008), and *Skyfall* (2012).

★ By way of comparison, the *Star Trek* franchise is much more family-friendly. The sci-fi adventures are spinoffs of the original *Star Trek* TV series and its years-later follow-up, *Star Trek: The Next Generation.* And while the movies do have violence, and sometimes profanity, and, especially in the later films, occasional sexual innuendo, it's generally pretty mild, much cleaner than even most contemporary television shows, and certainly softer than the James Bond pictures. The first of the big-screen movies, *Star Trek—The*

Motion Picture (1979), is rated G (though it contains some mild profanity and veiled nudity), and all of the sequels from the original-cast years (starring William Shatner, etc.) are rated PG: *Star Trek II: The Wrath of Khan* (1982), *Star Trek III: The Search for Spock* (1984), *Star Trek IV: The Voyage Home* (1986), *Star Trek V: The Final Frontier* (1989), *Star Trek VI: The Undiscovered Country* (1991), and *Star Trek: Generations* (1994).

The latter film passes the baton to the *Next Generation* cast (led by Patrick Stewart), leading to three more films: *Star Trek: First Contact* (1996, the first *Star Trek* movie to be rated PG-13), *Star Trek: Insurrection* (1998, PG) and *Star Trek: Nemesis* (2002, PG-13). The 2009 reboot, *Star Trek*, which is much more violent and sexual, and which has more profanity (including the f-word in the lyric of a song), is rated PG-13, and in terms of content might, arguably, be more comparable to the Bond films. A sequel to the reboot was released in 2013.

Clearly, these are all movies aimed at adults, and their PG (or M or GP) ratings did nothing to hinder their success at the box office.

MORE PG-RATED FILMS OBVIOUSLY MEANT FOR ADULTS

(in the days before PG-13):

★ The sex comedy *The Owl and the Pussycat* (1970), Barbra Streisand's fourth movie and first non-musical, which was originally rated R for language, but was edited, toned down, and received a PG.

★ George Lucas' first big hit, *American Graffiti* (1973), the teen comedy about cruising streets of Los Angeles in 1962, with profanity and a scene where some characters are mooning through car windows (and the 1979 sequel added Vietnam war violence, but still earned a PG).

★ The sex farce *A Touch of Class* (1973), which won Glenda Jackson the best-actress Oscar, with foul language and sex.

★ *The Sting* (1973), the Paul Newman-Robert Redford Oscar-winning classic con-artist comedy, with violence, foul language, and sexual suggestiveness.

★ Disaster flicks *The Towering Inferno* (1974), with Paul Newman, Steve McQueen, and an all-star cast stuck in a high-rise that catches fire, with implied sex, foul language, and many unpleasant, bloody deaths, and *Earthquake* (1974), with Charlton Heston leading an all-star cast trapped in various places during a Los Angeles earthquake, which features a lot of bloody mayhem, foul language, some innuendo, and an attempted rape.

★ The adultery comedy *Same Time, Next Year* (1978), with wall-to-wall sex talk and innuendo, as well as other foul language, and which has Ellen Burstyn uttering the f-word twice, once in a sexual context, which triggered an automatic R, but on appeal the film was given a PG with no changes.

★ The action-comedy *Hooper* (1978), with Burt Reynolds as a stuntman, a film that is pretty raunchy, with sex, nudity, and language, as well as the expected violence.

★ *Nine to Five* (1980), the workplace comedy with Jane Fonda, Dolly Parton and Lily Tomlin, laced with profanity, vulgarity, sexual innuendo, and marijuana smoking.

★ *Arthur* (1981), a 1930s-style screwball farce with Dudley Moore as a rich drunk living a carefree life, with quite a few vulgar gags and profanity.

- ★ *Mommie Dearest* (1981), the allegedly true story of actress Joan Crawford (Faye Dunaway) as a histrionic child-beating mother, with abusive violence, sex, and language.

- ★ *On Golden Pond* (1981), with Katharine Hepburn, Henry Fonda and Jane Fonda, an adaptation of the popular play about a father-daughter reconciliation, which has Jane Fonda in revealing clothing and a lot of profanity (which was a bit of a shock to older moviegoers, and the language has continued to surprise video renters in the years since).

- ★ The popular pop-music dance hit *Footloose* (1984), with vulgarity, foul language, and locker-room nudity.

- ★ *Ghostbusters* (1984), the hit supernatural comedy with Bill Murray and Dan Aykroyd, which has several sexual gags and other vulgarisms, along with profanity.

Some films that received M or GP ratings early on and were later re-rated when reissued in theaters or released on home video, were apparently judged by CARA to be a bit too harsh to remain in the PG category the second time around, and instead earned PG-13s, including *The Abominable Dr. Phibes* (1971), a horror-comedy starring Vincent Price; *Big Jake* (1971), a John Wayne western; *The Hospital* (1971), a dark satire of the medical profession, starring George C. Scott; and the Neil Simon anthology comedy *Plaza Suite* (1971), with Walter Matthau in three roles.

But even after the advent of the PG-13 rating, occasional movies continued to be rated PG when they were obviously very adult in terms of content.

FILMS RATED PG WITH ADULT CONTENT

(post PG-13):

★ The Oscar-winner *Out of Africa* (1985), with Meryl Streep and Robert Redford, which has a sex scene and an array of adult themes.

★ The movie that made Tom Cruise a superstar, *Top Gun* (1986), which has violence, sexual content, and a lot of profanity.

★ *3 Men and a Baby* (1987), with sex talk, profanity, and an unfortunate drug-dealer subplot (the 1990 sequel, *3 Men and a Little Lady* tones it down some and is also rated PG).

★ *Moonstruck* (1987), which won the best-actress Oscar for Cher and includes a sexual encounter and some profanity.

★ *Runaway Bride* (1999), with Julia Roberts and Richard Gere reunited after the success of the R-rated *Pretty Woman* (1990), this time with just enough language and sex talk to retain a PG.

★ The Goldie Hawn comedy *Overboard* (1987), which might seem at first glance to be a family film (and it was sold that way), with Hawn as a wealthy snob who loses her memory and is tricked by a blue-collar widower into becoming the mother to his rowdy brood of kids. And most of the film, despite the slightly off-putting premise, is family-friendly. But there is also quite a bit of profanity, along with sexual innuendo, implied sex, and Hawn wearing barely-there, extremely revealing outfits.

- ★ The comedy *Baby Boom* (1987), starring Diane Keaton as a professional woman suddenly saddled with an infant, a film with implied sex, profanity, and a partially nude babysitter.

- ★ *Roxanne* (1987), Steve Martin's modern twist on *Cyrano de Bergerac*, with sexual vulgarisms and a (mostly veiled) nude scene.

- ★ *Twins* (1988), a comedy about Arnold Schwarzenegger and Danny DeVito as twins separated at birth, with sexual contact, partial nudity, and lots of sex talk. A sequel titled *Triplets* is on the way.

- ★ *Beetle Juice* (1988), Tim Burton's fantasy-comedy starring Michael Keaton, has quite a bit of vulgarity and the f-word, which was supposedly automatic-PG-13 territory, even in the 1980s.

- ★ *Who Framed Roger Rabbit* (1988), the live-action/animated feature that lampoons classic cartoons of the 1930s and '40s, is another film made for adults but sold to children, with way too much adult material for kids, including violence, sexuality, foul language, and vulgarity, albeit with some of it veiled in comical ways.

- ★ *Steel Magnolias* (1989), featuring an all-star cast in intersecting stories of women in the South, with profanity and sexual innuendo.

- ★ *Dead Poets Society* (1989), a drama with comedy that stars Robin Williams as an English professor at a boys school encouraging their independence, with profanity, vulgarity, and an off-camera suicide.

★ *The Three Musketeers* (1993), the Disney *Young Guns*-style version with Charlie Sheen and Kiefer Sutherland, features sexuality, nudity, foul language, and a lot of violence, including innocent people being killed.

★ *A League of Their Own* (1992), the true story of a 1940s women's baseball league, with Geena Davis heading an all-star cast, and which contains a lot of profanity and vulgar, sexual talk.

One of the most popular films of the 1980s was *Big* (1988), the Tom Hanks fantasy-comedy about a young boy who wishes himself into

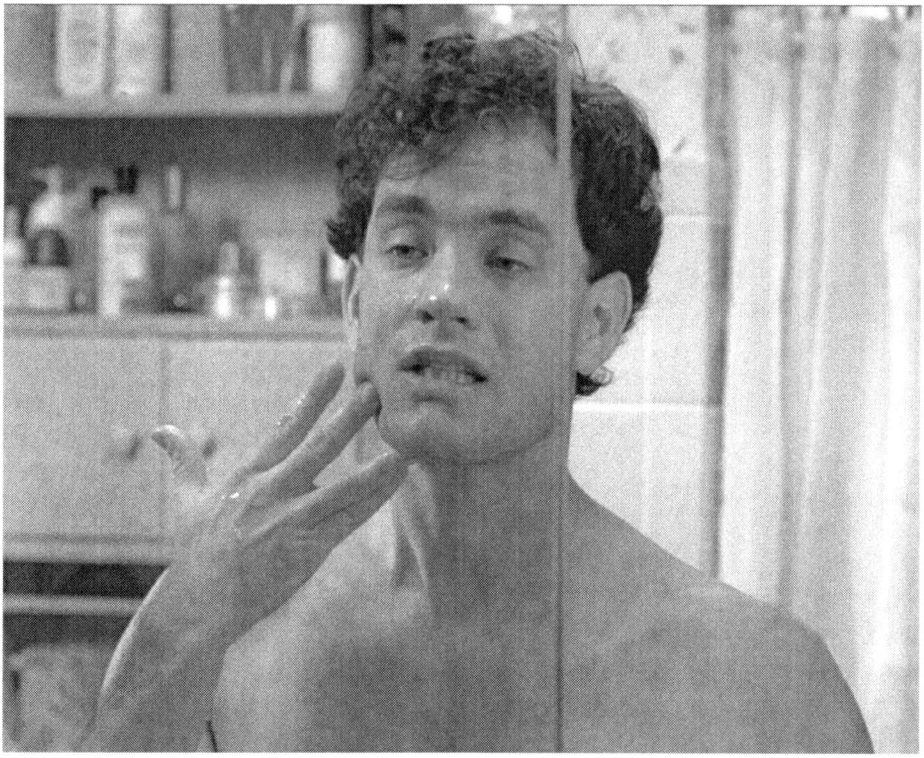

Tom Hanks in Penny Marshall's Big *(1988) —Twentieth Century Fox*

adulthood, though he retains the mind of a pre-adolescent. That PG-rated film includes sexual innuendo and profanity, including the f-word. There were several similarly plotted comedies released within months of each other, aimed at young audiences, but the others had young people switching bodies with adults. One of these was *18 Again!* (1988), with elderly George Burns and teenage Charlie Schlatter swapping physical forms, and it included the expected comic vulgarity, including close-ups of Burns' much-younger, bosomy, scantily-clad girlfriend, along with an especially inappropriate nude scene in an art class.

On the other end of the spectrum, there are occasionally PG-rated movies that make you wonder why in the world they weren't rated G. The best-picture Oscar-winner of 1982, *Chariots of Fire*, is one of those. Why in the world is it rated PG instead of G since there is nothing at all offensive in terms of content, save the words "bloody" (a British curse word) and "hell," each spoken once? In 1981, I wrote that this was "the first film I've seen that seems to completely defy its own PG rating; if ever there was a G-rated movie, it is *Chariots of Fire*." Watching it again today, I feel the same way.

PG FILMS THAT ARE CLEANER THAN AVERAGE:

- ★ *Heaven Can Wait* (1978), Warren Beatty's fantasy-comedy remake of *Here Comes Mr. Jordan*, which has a couple of mild cuss words.

- ★ *The Hunt for Red October* (1990), the submarine thriller with Sean Connery and Alec Baldwin, with a few profanities and some mild or off-camera violence.

- ★ *Father of the Bride* (1991), a remake of the 1950 family comedy, this time starring Steve Martin and Diane Keaton as parents of a young bride-to-be, a film with just a single vulgar comment. (The 1995 sequel, *Father of the Bride, Part II*, is also rated PG and has a few more vulgar gags than the first.)

★ *Sleepless in Seattle* (1993), with Tom Hanks and Meg Ryan as romantics destined to be together, with a small amount of profanity and vulgarity.

★ *Remember the Titans* (2000), in which Denzel Washington integrates a 1971 high school basketball team, with some profanity and violence.

★ *Snow Dogs* (2002), a family film from Disney with dentist Cuba Gooding Jr. inheriting the title animals.

Things have changed in the 21st century as the vast majority of PG-rated films are now aimed directly at youngsters.

RECENT PG MOVIES AIMED AT CHILDREN:

2010

★ Animated: *How to Train Your Dragon, The Secret of Kells, Despicable Me, Alpha and Omega, Megamind*, and *Tangled.* (The year's biggest film, the cartoon *Toy Story 3*, and the live-action *Ramona and Beezus* both had G ratings.)

★ Live-action: *The Spy Next Door, Tooth Fairy, Percy Jackson & The Olympians: The Lightning Thief, Diary of a Wimpy Kid, The Last Song, The Perfect Game, Furry Vengeance, Marmaduke, The Last Airbender, Standing Ovation, Nanny McPhee Returns, Expecting Mary, Flipped, The Nutcracker in 3D, Cats & Dogs: The Revenge of Kitty Galore, Yogi Bear*, and *Gulliver's Travels.*

2011

★ Animated: *The Illusionist* (a French film), *Rango, Mars Needs Moms, Arthur Christmas, Hoodwinked Too! Hood Vs. Evil, Kung Fu Panda 2, Puss in Boots, Happy Feet Two, The Adventures of Tintin*, and two films that combine animation with live action, *The Smurfs* and *Hop.*

- ★ Live-action: *Diary of a Wimpy Kid: Rodrick Rules, Judy Moody and the Not Bummer Summer, Mr. Popper's Penguins, Monte Carlo, Zookeeper, Spy Kids: All the Time in the World,* and the more entire-family-oriented *Dolphin Tale* and *The Muppets.*

2012

- ★ Animated: *The Lorax, Hotel Transylvania, Frankenweenie, Pirates! Band of Misfits, Brave, Ice Age: Continental Drift, ParaNorman, Madagascar 3: Europe's Most Wanted, Wreck-It Ralph,* and *Rise of the Guardians.*
- ★ Live-action: *Mirror, Mirror, Journey 2: The Mysterious Island, The Three Stooges, Diary of a Wimpy Kid: Dog Days,* and *Here Comes the Boom.*

RECENT PG MOVIES FOR ADULTS:

2010

- ★ From major studios: *Leap Year, Extraordinary Measures, Just Wright, Letters to Juliet, The Sorcerer's Apprentice, You Again, Mao's Last Dancer, Secretariat,* and *Tron Legacy.*
- ★ Independent productions: *Cairo Time, Princess Kaiulani, The Secrets of Jonathan Sperry,* and *Letters to God,* the latter two being faith films.
- ★ Documentaries: *Waiting for Superman, Babies, The Wildest Dream: Conquest of Everest, Countdown to Zero, Waking Sleeping Beauty, Cool It,* and *Ready, Set, Bag.*

(For the purpose of perspective, consider that there were sixty-something PG-13s and more than a hundred rated R that went into general release around the country in 2010.)

2011

- ★ From major studios: *The Big Year, Johnny English Reborn, Jack and Jill,* and *Hugo.*

- Independent productions: *Meek's Cutoff* and *Soul Surfer.*

2012

- From major studios: *Won't Back Down*, *Chasing Mavericks, Life of Pi,* and *Parental Guidance.*
- Independent productions: *16-Love* and *Cowgirls N' Angels.*

Also released in 2012 were *Unicorn City*, *Unitards,* and *Chick Magnets*, three independent PG films aimed at teens.

In 2012, two live-action films were big surprises that bucked the system— PG-rated family pictures in the best sense—movies that kids and adults can enjoy together.

The first was *Big Miracle*, the true story of a family of California whales that finds itself trapped in a threatening Arctic ice covering, with an all-star cast that includes John Krasinski, Drew Barrymore, Ted Danson, and Kristen Bell. *Big Miracle* is rated PG "for language," and there is a bit too much foul language for a film like this, though I would still put it in the family-friendly category.

The second was Disney's *The Odd Life of Timothy Green*, which could easily be rated G. A whimsical fable about an infertile couple (Jennifer Garner, Joel Edgerton) that writes down all the qualities they'd wish for their child, buries the papers in a box in the backyard garden and within hours finds that a 10-year-old boy (CJ Adams) has magically sprouted up to become their child. The film is rated PG "for mild thematic elements and brief language." The only foul language in the film is the word "hell" uttered once. The themes are about living a full life, seeking and giving love, along with death and loss—just like all of Disney's classic films dating back to the 1930s, films that easily earned G ratings. For that matter, the same themes are in *Toy Story 3*, which earned a G in 2010.

So here's the thing, when the ratings were just G, PG, and R, it essentially meant that a G-rated film was suitable for everyone, a PG-rated film might have some "mature" material, and, therefore, parents should use "parental guidance" before allowing a child to see it, and, of course, an R-rated film was for adults only. But somewhere along the way, the folks who make movies began balking at ratings for certain films because of some kind of perception that audiences were weeding out movies based on their ratings. Is it more likely, as suggested by Jack Valenti in Chapter 2, that most people just decide they want to see a certain film and then check out the rating secondarily, if at all?

Chapter 6

THE G RATING

On the Verge of Extinction

If the PG rating is endangered, the G is hanging by its fingernails on the edge of the cliff. The annual number of PG-rated movies has dropped dramatically over the years, especially since the PG-13 came on the scene, but G-rated movies have dropped off much further.

In 1968, the first year of the rating system, there were many G-rated films for adults in movie houses. Mature audiences had choices from every genre and themes that were clearly not aimed at children, yet these films were generally as clean as any movie from the 1940s. And many of these films earned accolades from critics and the public, and were among the top box-office draws. In fact, 1968's two biggest hits, Barbra Streisand's Oscar-winning film debut in *Funny Girl* and Stanley Kubrick's seminal science-fiction epic *2001: A Space Odyssey*, carry G ratings. The latter is squeaky-clean, without any offensive content, and *Funny Girl* has only the words "damn" and "hell," each spoken once.

Other adult movies that also received G ratings during that first year did have a bit more adult material—dialogue might contain the occasional "damn" or "hell," along with some mildly vulgar jokes, usually innuendo, and violence might be portrayed that was not overly graphic but still might show a bit of blood being spilled, and there could be nudity if it was not shown in a sexual manner.

MORE G-RATED MOVIES FOR ADULTS RELEASED IN 1968:

- ★ The sci-fi classic *Planet of the Apes*, starring Charlton Heston as the leader of a crew of astronauts who have apparently landed on another planet where apes rule over humans. The film contains most of the aforementioned elements—violence, nudity, profanity. Most of the sequels in the original franchise are also rated G: Only one of the five movies in the original *Planet of the Apes* film series released between 1968 and 1973 is not rated G, the fourth, *Conquest of the Planet of the Apes*, which earned a PG. (Tim Burton's 2001 remake of *Planet of the Apes* carries a PG-13, as does the 2011 "reboot" *Rise of the Planet of the Apes.*)

- ★ Neil Simon's comedy *The Odd Couple*, scripted by Simon from his play about two disparate divorced men who become reluctant roommates. Walter Matthau re-created his Broadway role as the slovenly Oscar Madison, and his frequent movie co-star, Jack Lemmon, played fussy neatnik Felix Unger. The film contains some profanity and a few vulgar jokes, including dancers in skimpy outfits in a nightclub. (The 30-years-later sequel, also written by Simon, and starring Matthau and Lemmon, is rated PG-13 for sexuality and language, including the f-word spoken twice.)

- ★ John Wayne's Vietnam War movie *The Green Berets*, which he directed and in which he stars as a colonel who assembles a team of Green Berets for a tour in Vietnam, has the bloody violence you would expect in a film about men at war, as well as some profanity.

- ★ *The Subject Was Roses*, based on the Pulitzer Prize-winning play, with Martin Sheen and Oscar-winner Jack Albertson, reprising their Broadway roles as father and son, and with Patricia Neal as the wife and mother, in the story of a young World War II veteran trying in vain to connect with his disconnected parents, with some adult language.

- ★ John Wayne's firefighting epic *Hellfighters*, with Jim Hutton and Katharine Ross, is about men who fight dangerous oil-well fires, with profanity and violence.

- ★ *Ice Station Zebra*, a Cold War thriller with Rock Hudson taking a nuclear sub to the North Pole, encountering intrigue and a variety of disparate characters at each other's throats, contains some violence and language.

- ★ Fred Astaire's last musical, *Finian's Rainbow*, is a comedy-fantasy about an Irishman stealing a pot o' gold from a leprechaun (Tommy Steele), then heading for the American South to plant it and watch it grow, literally. Mostly whimsical, but with some sharp satire pointed at race relations during this era of the rise of civil rights, and some profanity.

- ★ *The Heart Is a Lonely Hunter* is an adaptation of the Carson McCullers sentimental novel about a deaf mute (Alan Arkin) who touches the lives of several troubled souls in a small Southern town, though none detect that he has troubles of his own, with some very adult themes.

- And perhaps most surprising on this list, the Hammer horror film *Dracula Has Risen From the Grave*, marking Christopher Lee's second outing as the title character, and, as with others in the franchise, a film that is notable for taking the bloodsucking count out of the tame black-and-white era and flaunting sex and blood in color. The sex is off-camera and there is no nudity, but there is a fair amount of bloody violence.

The significance of all these movies being rated G is compounded when you remember that the ratings didn't go into effect until quite late in 1968. Since no successive year, even 1969, has had nearly as many adult movies rated G, it becomes apparent that first, the CARA board members were still feeling their way around the ratings, deciding what constituted a G or PG or R, and second, that these movies were made before the ratings were in place, and the filmmakers were simply out to entertain in hopes that their films would find an audience, unaware and unconcerned about what the ratings might mean. It wasn't long, however, before the filmmakers and the studios began to seek out a certain demographic by pursuing a particular rating. By early 1969, films were already being made with ratings in mind.

We still saw a few G-rated movies aimed at adults that second year of the ratings, including the western that became John Wayne's Oscar-winner, *True Grit*; the European-tour farce *If It's Tuesday, This Must Be Belgium*; the sci-fi melodrama *Marooned*, about astronauts unable to return to Earth, starring Gregory Peck; James Garner's comedy western *Support Your Local Sheriff*; Neil Simon's comedy *The Out of Towners*, starring Jack Lemmon; and three musicals—*Sweet Charity*, with Shirley MacLaine; the song-filled version of *Goodbye, Mr. Chips*, starring Peter O'Toole and Petula Clark; and Barbra Streisand's *Hello, Dolly*! co-starring Walter Matthau.

But many more 1969 movies, which might have refrained from bloodier violence or offensive cuss words or dirtier jokes before the ratings came into play, were now including just a smidgen of this kind of stronger material in order to stay out of the G-rated pool. Why? Because the G was quickly coming to be perceived as the rating for movies aimed at children. The vast majority of G-rated movies were—not surprisingly—from Disney, animated features and live-action films made specifically for a young audience (*The Aristocats*, *The Love Bug*).

Whether the G was really perceived by the public as the rating for children's movies is certainly debatable, but there's no question that the studios thought so. As Hollywood's movers and shakers were ever on the watch for a way to lay the blame for underperforming movies on something other than a film's quality, they found a convenient scapegoat in the ratings.

Still, there were quite a few popular grown-up G-rated movies

John Wayne and Kim Darby in Henry Hathaway's True Grit *(1969) —Paramount*

released throughout the 1970s, some of which are as clean as they can be, while others are surprisingly adult in their approach, with violence, profanity (mostly of the "hell" and "damn" variety), sexual innuendo, fleeting nudity, etc.—and many were huge box-office hits, despite the dreaded G rating.

G-RATED FILMS FOR ADULTS FROM THE 1970s

- ★ The all-star terror-in-the-air picture *Airport* (1970), which single-handedly launched the disaster-movie trend of the 1970s.
- ★ *Tora! Tora! Tora!* (1970), the well-regarded World War II epic that relates events leading up to the bombing of Pearl Harbor from both the American and Japanese points of view.
- ★ The John Wayne westerns *Chisum* and *Rio Lobo* (1970).
- ★ Blake Edwards and Julie Andrews' wartime musical *Darling Lili* (1970).
- ★ Elaine May's dark comedy *A New Leaf*, with Walter Matthau (1971).
- ★ The Steve McQueen racing movie *Le Mans* (1971).
- ★ The contemporary Sherlock Holmes satire *They Might Be Giants* (1971).
- ★ The beloved musical *Fiddler on the Roof* (1971).
- ★ Peter Bogdanovich's screwball farce *What's Up, Doc?* (1972), starring Barbra Streisand.
- ★ *Sounder* (1972), a story of black sharecroppers in the 1930s (and its 1976 sequel, *Part 2, Sounder*).

- The musical remake of *Lost Horizon* (1973).

- Blake Edwards and Peter Sellers' Inspector Clouseau sequel *Return of the Pink Panther* (1975), the only film in the franchise not rated PG.

- *The Wiz* (1978), the urban musical interpretation of *The Wizard of Oz,* starring Diana Ross and Michael Jackson.

- The pensive, lovingly told story of a young boy and a horse stranded on a desert island, *The Black Stallion* (1979).

- The first *Star Trek* movie (1979).

Another aspect to consider is the number of older movies made before CARA was in place that received ratings for the first time when they went into theatrical reissues after 1968 or were released on home video. In 1971, for example, the most popular movie of all time, the Civil War epic *Gone With the Wind* (1939), was rated for a theatrical reissue and received a G, despite its embedded themes of wartime violence, illicit sex, and possible rape, however discreetly they were portrayed (and which were probably considered coy and inoffensive by the 1970s rating board, especially in the context of the kind of movies they were watching day in and day out). *Gone With the Wind* also has Clark Gable as Rhett Butler using the word "damn" near the end of the film (which caused quite a stir in 1939), as well as a famous scene of dozens of dead and dying soldiers laid out on the ground as a striking camera shot pulls back to reveal just how devastating a toll the war has left.

Another blockbuster that received a belated G rating (in 1969) is the 1959 multiple Oscar-winner *Ben-Hur*, starring Charlton Heston, which features quite a bit of bloody violence in battles on land and sea, including beatings and whippings; the famous chariot race, in which one character falls to the ground and is run over by a chariot, and another is dragged a considerable distance as his flesh is ripped; and, of course, the crucifixion of Jesus.

Then there was Elizabeth Taylor's infamous role as *Cleopatra* (1963), a film that shows quite a bit of violence, including spurting blood, and a considerable amount of female nudity, though not as graphically portrayed as it would be today, yet earned a G rating for its 1971 reissue.

Other golden oldies that earned G ratings upon being reissued include *Mary Poppins* (1964), *The Sound of Music* (1965), *My Fair Lady* (1964), *Around the World in Eighty Days* (1956), and *The Wizard of Oz* (1939).

The enormous success of these films provides irrefutable evidence that moviegoers are just on the lookout for good movies, and they are not likely to avoid a film because it carries a G rating. Yet, filmmakers

Julie Andrews and the children in Robert Wise's The Sound of Music *(1965) — Twentieth Century Fox*

continued—and continue—to look for ways to manipulate the system by slipping something in, sometimes seemingly as an afterthought, to muddy the waters of a G-level film just enough to push it into either the PG or PG-13 category.

By the end of the 1970s, adult movies with G ratings were all but finished, and as the 1980s kicked in, the G category was overwhelmingly dominated by animated features and documentaries, the latter gaining ground as IMAX theaters began to pop up around the country. These days, IMAX theaters are everywhere and screen a variety of mainstream movies, providing a venue for an outsized alternative experience with Hollywood movies in both 3D and "flat" or "2D" formats. But early on these mega-size screens were exclusive to big cities and had in their rotation a variety of eye-popping short documentaries (generally forty to forty-five minutes in length), many of them travelogues featuring historical re-creations with actors.

Of course, many documentaries fall into each of the PG, PG-13, or R rating categories as well, depending on the subject matter and the director's sensibilities. Similarly, more and more animated features are throwing in vulgar gags that ensure PG ratings, and a few go even further to earn a PG-13.

But animated and documentary films still dominate the G-rated arena, along with a fairly recent niche that has risen out of the independent filmmaking movement, the so-called "faith" or "Christian" genre—very clean adult/family films that feature a religious component, usually of Christian beliefs. The main thing all movies in this genre have in common is a strong moral message, and while some can be quite heavy-handed, the better examples bury the message in a compelling story with universal appeal. Some of these films have serious themes that earn PG or PG-13 ratings, but most are rated G and carry that banner unashamedly.

RECENT G-RATED MOVIES

2010

★ Animated: *Toy Story 3*, the biggest movie of the year.

- ★ Live-action: *Ramona and Beezus.*
- ★ Documentary: *Oceans* and *Hubble 3-D.*

2011

- ★ Animated: *Gnomeo and Juliet, Rio, Cars 2, Winnie the Pooh,* and *Alvin and the Chipmunks: Chip-Wrecked* (There was also a reissue of Disney's 1994 *The Lion King* in 3D.).
- ★ Documentary/Concert movies: *Justin Bieber: Never Say Never, Lord of the Dance, African Cats,* and *Cave of Forgotten Dreams.*
- ★ Christian Independent: *Seven Days in Utopia* and *The Mighty Macs.*

2012

- ★ Animated: *The Secret World of Arrietty*, a Japanese film dubbed in English and distributed by Disney, and the Russian *Space Dogs 3D*, dubbed in English and released independently. (Disney also reissued three of its G-rated animated classics in 3D, 1991's *Beauty and the Beast* and the Pixar films *Finding Nemo* from 2003 and 2001's *Monsters, Inc.*).
- ★ Live action (with puppets): *The Oogieloves in the Big Balloon Adventure.*
- ★ Documentary: *The Whale*, about an isolated baby Orca; Disneynature's annual Earth Day film, *Chimpanzee*, about an isolated baby chimp; and *To the Arctic 3D*, a forty-minute IMAX picture about a mother polar bear and her two cubs.

In 2010 of the fortysomething PG-rated movies released "wide" in theaters all over the country, the vast majority were aimed at kids/families (most of them animated), with fewer than ten aimed squarely at an adult audience. And there were sixty-something PG-13s and more than a hundred films rated R.

And so it goes. There's a trend at work, and the rating board is playing into it, declining to dole out Gs like it used to. To delve a bit further, let's backtrack and look at the animation explosion of the 1990s. It actually began in 1989 with *The Little Mermaid*, which signaled that Disney was back on track in terms of creative quality, with animated features that adults and children could enjoy equally. And in short order, Disney's next few cartoon movies were equally successful in both artistic and commercial terms—*Beauty and the Beast* (1991), *Aladdin* (1992), and *The Lion King* (1994), and all were rated G.

Other G-rated animation from Disney during the 1990s—*The Rescuers Down Under* (1990), *Pocahontas* (1995), *The Hunchback of Notre Dame* (1996), *Hercules* (1997), *Mulan* (1998), and *Tarzan* (1999)—did well enough at the box office, in varying degrees, but the earlier four were the titles that helped Disney regain its crown as king of animation. After *The Lion King*, however, a new kid on the block, making headway with a new kind of animation, would overshadow Disney in a big way.

That, of course, would be Pixar, which released its first feature-length, computer-animated cartoon, *Toy Story*, in 1995, and has had an unprecedented run of enormous box-office success with thirteen movies in seventeen years, not one of them claiming less than blockbuster status. Perhaps even more surprising is that, with one exception, Pixar's movies have also been universally embraced by critics, which is rare indeed. The exception is *Cars 2* (2011), and even that one was a commercial hit.

Not that anyone over at Walt's place ever really saw any of this as competition, since Disney was the distributor for all the Pixar features up to 2006, and in that year Disney purchased Pixar, formally making it part of the Mouse House family.

Pixar's first five movies were rated G: *Toy Story* (1995), A Bug's Life (1998), *Toy Story 2* (1999), *Monsters, Inc.* (2001), and *Finding Nemo* (2003). In 2004, *The Incredibles* became Pixar's first PG-rated movie. The next three reverted to G ratings: *Cars* (2006), *Ratatouille* (2007) and *WALL-E* (2008). Then came *Up* (2009), which earned a PG rating, followed by the G-rated *Toy Story 3* (2010) and *Cars 2* (2011).

In 2012, Pixar's thirteenth movie, *Brave*, was given the studio's third PG rating.

So why were *The Incredibles*, *Up*, and *Brave* each rated PG instead of G? Here are CARA's brief explanations displayed with the ratings, keeping in mind that these are cartoons and what is shown is not realistically portrayed:

- ★ *The Incredibles*: "Rated PG for action violence." There is a fair amount of violence here, from fistfights to explosions, along with some mildly vulgar innuendo and a couple of mild cuss words.

- ★ *Up*: "Rated PG for some peril and action." This film also features violence, albeit much less and much milder than what is depicted in *The Incredibles*. There is no off-color language or sexual innuendo here, though some of the themes are clearly adult in an emotional sense. (Good luck watching the first ten minutes without tearing up.)

- ★ *Brave*: "Rated PG for some scary action and rude humor." Action may be equated with violence here, since a character loses his leg to an animal, and there is some mild vulgarity, a humorous moment with brief implied nudity (not shown) and another regarding a buxom woman's cleavage.

Here's the real question: Are these three movies any rougher or more intense than Disney's early classics, such as *Snow White and the Seven Dwarfs* (1937), with its scary witch, poison apple, and spooky imagery in the forest? Or *Pinocchio* (1940), in which one character is transformed into a donkey and the protagonist is swallowed by a whale and appears to have drowned? Or *Fantasia* (1940), with its dancing demons and ghosts, snarling dinosaurs, mildly vulgar cupids, and naked female centaurs? Or *Bambi* (1942), in which the title character's mother is killed by hunters and a ferocious forest fire is depicted? Or

Peter Pan (1953), with pirates, swordfights, a kidnapping, a man-eating crocodile, and a near drowning of a young woman tied to a post? None of these, nor any of Disney's other pre-1969 animated films, were rated when initially released, of course, but they did receive ratings years later when they were reissued in theaters, and each earned a G. And all were quite successful—especially with theatrical re-releases, and more recently on DVD and Blu-ray.

All of the moments described above seem intrinsic to the stories portrayed in these various films and are mostly shown in subtle or broad cartoony ways, so I am not suggesting that any of them should have been rated PG, but it must be said that G-rated movies for kids often contain edgy material when examined from a child's point of

Merida, voiced by Kelly MacDonald in Brave *(2012) —Disney/Pixar*

view (as alluded to by Steven Spielberg in Chapter 4). Today, however, animation filmmakers, for the most part, tend to throw in some vulgar gags, scatological or flatulence humor, or something else that they feel will guarantee their film being bumped from G to PG.

On the other hand, *Bully* notwithstanding, most documentary filmmakers don't seem to care what rating they get—G, PG, PG-13, R, whatever. Since the vast majority of theatrical documentaries are not aimed at young audiences, the people who make these movies generally appear to be content with whatever ratings land on their films.

After Pixar made inroads into the animated-feature market, most of the other major studios (and some independents) also began producing computer-animated films on a regular basis, and now we get several each year that are non-Disney/non-Pixar products. And most of those seem to reach for the PG rating by including something vulgar, which is the kind of content that many parents find inappropriate for their children. They may put up with it and even purchase the film on DVD/Blu-ray later, but they don't like it, especially while their kids are watching it over and over and over.

Several studio chiefs have been quoted over the past couple of decades about why they deliberately avoid the G rating, arguing that it turns off teenagers and, after all, teens are the major target audience for modern motion pictures. But movies don't get to be huge hits without going beyond that narrow target audience. Similarly, a G-rated film doesn't become a really big hit without expanding beyond half-price children's tickets.

Take *Toy Story 3* in 2010; an animated film, yes, but that movie was the biggest hit of the year, and not just because families with children attended. In 2008, *WALL-E* and *Horton Hears a Who!* were G-rated films among the top-ten biggest moneymakers of the year. Similarly, *The Polar Express* (2004) and *Finding Nemo* (2003) were in the top ten of their respective years. That's an awful lot of tickets sold.

In 1995, the comedy *Babe* was a big hit, and at first glance it would seem to be a picture that is strictly for children—a G-rated, live-action comedy about barnyard animals that talk. But it also appealed to adults and teens and everyone in-between. It was clever and smart, and very funny, raising the bar quite high for live-action family fare that truly appeals to every member of the family. Because *Babe* was such a big hit, it obviously drew on an audience that went far beyond the toddler set.

While it's easy to credit Universal Pictures' smart marketing strategy with the movie's success—remember those funny, memorable TV ad spots featuring the title character singing "La-la-LA!"—what really made *Babe* a hit was word-of-mouth praise from the audience. *Babe* so utterly charmed every age that people were telling their friends, "You've got to see this movie."

I'm pretty sure no one ever said, "I'd recommend this movie to you if only it wasn't rated G." But because several other family movies failed over the next few years, Hollywood forgot the lesson taught by *Babe* and again began looking for excuses. Those subsequent family films that were ignored by audiences were snubbed because they were bad movies, not because they were rated G. But try telling that to movie execs.

Sometimes modern movies do receive G ratings, even when they don't seem to deserve them, especially when compared to similar PG-rated movies that were rated around the same time. Take for example a pair of aquatic-themed animated features with different ratings that were coincidentally released on DVD the same day in 2007:

The Reef—which is sort of *Finding Nemo* meets *Shark Tale* with a sprinkling of *The Little Mermaid* and a shark that raps—was a straight-to-video release rated G, despite a multitude of body-function gags that seem wildly inappropriate for that rating. And *Surf's Up*, which at first glance appears to invite comparisons to *Happy Feet* since the main characters are penguins, but is really more of a surfing spoof, is rated PG for a bit of innuendo and language.

But in my opinion, *Surf's Up* is much less vulgar than *The Reef*. So why did *The Reef* get the G and *Surf's Up* the PG? That's anyone's guess, of course. But it does seem to validate the theory that on any given day the CARA board can shift from liberal to conservative, depending on who calls in sick or is on vacation and how many happen to show up for work that day.

Perhaps, the most preposterous aspect of all this is not just the notion that the G is a children's rating, but the implication that somehow making a movie "clean" will dumb it down or make it less compelling or thrilling or funny or scary. And even more idiotic is the idea that the G rating is box-office poison, as the examples above of so many G-rated box-office hits demonstrate.

Chapter 7

AFTER TWO DECADES CARA

Attempts to Explain Itself

Potentially offensive material identified by CARA for the purposes of awarding movie ratings ranges from language to violence to sex to nudity to drugs to smoking. Of course, this is an oversimplification since there are many shades of gray between those black-and-white descriptive terms. And if you look at those little boxes below the rating letter on movie posters and other advertising, you'll see vague, terse summaries that may leave you wondering a bit.

If it says rated R for language, for example, does it mean a few offensive expletives and nothing else? Or does it mean 150 usages of the f-word and a lot of other foul language throughout the film—profanity, obscenity, vulgarity, sexual innuendo? And does that mean there's no violence or sex or nudity, or are those things present but not mentioned because the board considers them to be at a PG level, unlike the R-level language? Sometimes, an effort is made to qualify these descriptions, but the result is often like a text message, concise at the expense of understandability.

CARA began dispensing brief explanations of R ratings in September 1990 and by early 1992, descriptions began showing up for PG and PG-13 films as well. Here's an explanation taken from the CARA website, www.filmratings.com:

> With the exception of G-rated films, which are deemed appropriate for all ages, contemporary ratings now feature brief explanatory phrases specific to that film and its rating. For example, [an] animated film received a PG rating for 'mild language and some crude humor,' while [another] was rated PG-13 for 'intense sequences of adventure violence, including frightening images.' These descriptions strive to convey cautionary content warnings parents may wish to consider. The ratings descriptor on [a] World War II film read rated R for 'intense prolonged realistically graphic sequences of war violence and for language.' Rating descriptions provide information to parents on the specific type of material in each movie that resulted in the rating so that the parent can decide if that content is appropriate to the individual maturity and sensitivities of their children.

The most recent change in the way the rating system looks at content came a few years ago when the Rating Board members began taking notice of smoking in movies:

> In 2007, in response to growing parental concerns, adult smoking was made a factor in the rating system. Youth smoking was always considered in a film's rating. This decision brought into the mix three additional questions: Is smoking pervasive in the film? Is it glamorized? Is there a historic, public health, or other mitigating context? Already, most films with smoking were rated R for other reasons, such as violence or sex. This move ensured an added layer of scrutiny and transparency. Now, for example, a film that portrayed a period in American history where smoking was ubiquitous

> might not see its rating increased due to the historic context, but it would likely include a rating descriptor of 'pervasive smoking' for parents to consider. The appearance of smoking in a motion picture does not require the assignment of any particular rating. Rather, it is a factor to be evaluated in the overall context of the motion picture.

During the 1970s, the first decade of the ratings, many filmmakers were pushing things just to see how far they could go, how much they could get away with, and X-rated films occasionally meandered into mainstream theaters. The highest-profile, best-remembered example is *Midnight Cowboy*, which won the best-picture Academy Award (along with two other Oscars) after its 1969 release. Two years later it was re-rated to an R. That happened with others as well, including *A Clockwork Orange* (1971), re-rated from X to R one year after its initial release, and *Last Tango in Paris* (1972), which was originally released with an X rating, then edited to earn an R in 1981, then re-rated in its original form in 1997 to receive its current NC-17 rating. On the other hand, the animated film *Fritz the Cat* (1972) kept and reveled in its X rating, using it as an advertising gimmick.

But it wasn't until the early 1980s that Hollywood mainstream movies really began to push the R rating as far as possible with violence and gore, sex and nudity, and foul language. Films such as the gangster movie *Scarface* (1983), which toned down the graphic gore on appeal to avoid an X rating, but set some kind of record for use of the f-word, and any number of horror/slasher movies from the *Halloween*, *Friday the 13th*, and *A Nightmare on Elm Street* franchises to *The Thing* (1982) and *Hellraiser* (1987), etc., helped gory sequences crawl out of the drive-ins and urban grind houses and into neighborhood theaters.

Scarface also helped the same happen with language. And excessive sex and nudity became more and more commonplace in comedies, thrillers, and action pictures, such as *Body Heat* (1983), *Trading*

Places (1983), *Blue Velvet* (1986), and many more. Sex and nudity also overtook a genre of R-rated movies about and aimed at teenagers, following up on the college-level hijinks of the enormously popular *National Lampoon's Animal House* (1978), with *Porky's* (1981) and its sequels, *Fast Times at Ridgemont High* (1982), *Revenge of the Nerds* (1984), etc.

Flipping the coin, there are also a number of movies that were rated R, but could easily have snagged PG ratings if they had not insisted on using the f-word a few too many times, such as two films directed by Robert Redford, *Ordinary People* (1980) and *The Milagro Beanfield War* (1988); the Richard Pryor comedies *Bustin' Loose* (1981) and *Moving* (1988); the Steve Martin/John Candy comedy *Planes, Trains & Automobiles* (1987); and the Tom Cruise/Jack Nicholson military thriller, *A Few Good Men* (1992).

On the other hand, there are often movies with PG or PG-13 ratings that make you wonder how they got away with that, considering the mature content: *Ragtime* (1981), *Sixteen Candles* (1984), *Forrest Gump* (1994), *Dumb & Dumber* (1994), *Anchorman: The Legend of Ron Burgundy* (2004), *The Break Up* (2006), *The Haunting in Connecticut* (2009), *An Education* (2009), *Drag Me to Hell* (2009), *Couples Retreat* (2009), *Insidious* (2010), *Hanna* (2011), *Crazy, Stupid, Love* (2011), *Sucker Punch* (2011), *Total Recall* (2012), etc.

A prestige film can sometimes get away with what seems a very soft rating for the level of mature content it employs. In 1987, *The Last Emperor* received a PG-13, but the film contains graphic violence, sex, nudity, opium use, and profanity, including the f-word once. The film went on to receive nine Academy Awards, including best picture. Another best-picture Oscar-winner was Kevin Costner's *Dances With Wolves* (1990), which has bloody violence, sex, and nudity that seems to go well beyond the PG-13 wall, but it nonetheless carries that rating.

The 1994 best-picture winner was *Forrest Gump*, also rated PG-13 "for drug content, some sensuality, and war violence," but that violence is pretty graphic, and the sexual material, including nudity, seems inappropriate for teens, while the drug content is both cocaine and heroin. And similar complaints can be made about content in subsequent PG-13 best-picture Oscar winners *Titanic* (1997), *A Beautiful Mind* (2001), *Chicago* (2002), and *Million Dollar Baby* (2004).

Historically, that is, immediately after the inception of the rating descriptions, nudity was often overlooked for some reason. Two 1991 examples are *The Doors*, with the R-rating explanation reading "for heavy drug content, and for strong sexuality and language." The film also has several graphic sex scenes and quite a bit of nudity. And *Billy Bathgate* is rated R "for some gangster violence and for language." No mention is made of the full-frontal nude scenes. Although it must be said that in recent years, the explanations have picked up on nudity more, in particular what is now often described as "graphic nudity" in R-rated films.

Sometimes, it's obvious that a studio doesn't have confidence in a sequel to an R-rated hit, so to widen the reach of the second or third or fourth film in an R-rated franchise, a softer rating is deliberately pursued.

PG OR PG-13 SEQUELS TO R-RATED FILMS:

★ *Conan the Destroyer* (1984, rated PG) and *Red Sonja* (1985, PG-13), both follow-ups to the R-rated *Conan the Barbarian* (1982).

★ *Amityville 3-D* (1983, PG) is the only one of nine *Amityville Horror* movies not rated R (including made-for-TV and straight-to-video sequels).

★ *Mad Max Beyond Thunderdome* (1985, PG-13) is a tamer follow-up to the R-rated *Mad Max* (1979) and *The Road Warrior* (1981).

- *Police Academy* (1984), a raunchy R-rated comedy, was followed by *Police Academy 2: Their First Assignment* (1985), which was rated PG-13, and five subsequent sequels that were each rated PG.

- *RoboCop 3* (1992, PG-13) followed two R-rated *RoboCops* (1987/1990).

- *Speed 2: Cruise Control* (1997, PG-13) is a sequel to the R-rated *Speed* (1994).

- *Be Cool* (2005) is a PG-13 sequel to the R-rated *Get Shorty* (1995).

- *Scary Movie 3* (2003, PG-13) and *Scary Movie 4* (2006, PG-13) are the only films not rated R in the four-film franchise (with another released in 2013).

- *Alien vs. Predator* (2004, PG-13), a sequel in the ten-film total (so far) *Alien* and *Predator* franchises, is the only one not rated R.

- *Terminator Salvation* (2009, PG-13) which followed three R-rated *Terminator* films (1984-2003).

- *Live Free or Die Hard* (2007, PG-13) came after three R-rated *Die Hard* movies (1988-95).

Those in charge of CARA have said repeatedly that movie ratings are not intended as a marketing tool, but the rest of Hollywood obviously feels differently. And CARA often plays into the game, as with a 2009 adjustment to those green cards or "bands," as they are referred to, that precede movie previews in theaters, online and on home video.

Just before the change, in January of that year, while waiting for a film to begin, I watched a pair of back-to-back trailers for two then-upcoming romantic comedies, *The Proposal*, with Sandra Bullock, and *The Ugly Truth*, with Katherine Heigl. And both trailers contained similar gags about sexual arousal that I was quite surprised to see in movie trailers preceded by that familiar green band that reads: "The following PREVIEW has been approved for ALL AUDIENCES by the Motion Picture Association of America." (The words "PREVIEW" and "ALL AUDIENCES" are in larger type because that's the way they appear on the green bands.)

Really? ALL audiences? Of ALL ages? True, the trailers' offending moments are innuendo, and younger children probably won't get the

Sandra Bullock and Ryan Reynolds in The Proposal *(2009) —Touchstone*

joke. But teens will. And although *The Proposal* was later released with a questionable PG-13 rating, *The Ugly Truth* was rightfully rated R. To my way of thinking, those gags had no place in trailers that the movie-raters had "approved for all audiences," to include young children. That's just crazy.

Around the same time, perhaps to respond to parents' concerns about such things, CARA took steps to prevent that from happening again. How, you ask? By banning such salacious gags from "all audience" trailers? No, that would be censorship (and make too much sense). Instead, the MPAA slightly redesigned the green band. Now, instead of "all audiences" it says "appropriate audiences." That's right. The green-band statement is now "The following PREVIEW has been approved for APPROPRIATE AUDIENCES . . ."

So what does that mean, you may well ask? After much deep thought and quite a bit of online research I can state with authority, "Who knows?" This change went into effect in early 2009 without any announcement from the CARA or the MPAA.

When I finally noticed it, I searched the Web for some explanation. The closest I came is an official e-mail gobbledygook response by MPAA vice president for corporate communications Elizabeth Kaltman to "Movie Mom" Nell Minow (http://blog.beliefnet.com/moviemom/): "(It was) intended to allow motion picture distributors and exhibitors greater freedom to accurately promote motion pictures to appropriate audiences while honoring our pledge to American parents that stronger advertising material will not reach inappropriate younger audiences. Whether a movie is rated G or PG, the appropriate audience tag still maintains that the trailer is appropriate for the viewing audience."

Say what? How does giving movie studios "greater freedom" allow the MPAA to honor its pledge to American parents? This also came on the heels of a speech given by Dan Glickman, MPAA president at the time, who told the Media Institute that the rating board is "working hard to make the system more transparent."

What's really transparent is that the MPAA, which pledges to watch out for our kids, is actually watching out for the movie studios

. . . not that that's a big surprise. So the MPAA apparently felt that the aforementioned sexual gags (and who knows what else) were appropriate for "all audiences." And now, the "appropriate audiences" label gives studios the go-ahead to push the boundaries even further.

These are a few of the most recent examples of the rating board's explanations, taken from summer 2012 weekly bulletins issued by CARA, followed by my observations about actual content:

★ *Snow White and the Huntsman:* "Rated PG-13 for intense sequences of violence and action, and brief sensuality." This revisionist take on the children's fairy tale has Snow White being taken advantage of by the evil queen who resents her beauty, but she eventually becomes an empowered warrior who fights back. The "violence and action" includes quite a bit of fighting, punching, kicking, slashing with swords, stabbing with arrows, and generally bloody battles resulting in a high body count. We also see the queen kill the king with a knife; she kills a bird, digs out its heart, and eats it; and she screams, yells, and threatens all sorts of mayhem. There are also various monsters and other fantasy creatures. The "brief sensuality" may refer to the naked queen, with only her bare back shown, as she descends into a bath of creamy white liquid, or perhaps, the form-fitting dresses that reveal cleavage. There is also some foul language.

★ *Madagascar 3: Europe's Most Wanted:* "Rated PG for some mild action and rude humor." Second sequel in the animated *Madagascar* franchise has the zoo animals linking up with a European circus while trying to get back to New York. There is a lot of action, including comic gunplay, though it isn't any more intense than any of the

G-rated Tom & Jerry or Bugs Bunny cartoons of old. The "rude humor" may refer to a few scatological jokes, such as vomiting, or, in keeping with the abstract nature of the animation art, to the enormous backside and large pointed breasts of the female villain, to which there are oblique references. There is also mild language, as when someone says "That's Bolshevik," an obvious euphemism for an expletive.

★ *Ice Age: Continental Drift:* "Rated PG for mild rude humor and action peril." Like *Madagascar 3*, this is a sequel to a successful animated franchise focusing on anthropomorphic animals, in this case creatures from the prehistoric Ice Age of the title.

Note the difference in phrasing of the two explanations for PG ratings. *Madagascar 3* has "mild action" and "rude humor," while *Continental Drift* has "mild rude humor" and "action peril." Actually, the films are comparable in terms of content. The difference between "rude humor" and "mild rude humor" must be miniscule, since it seemed to me about the same in each film. This one has several verbal double-entendres and some female characters are given humanistic physical traits, and similar euphemisms replace swearing, such as "Holy crab!" And the action is perhaps even more intense here since it includes a lot of earthquakes, falling rocks, breaking ice floes, etc. But *Madagascar 3* has gunplay and a villain threatening to kill the animals that are the film's protagonists.

★ *People Like Us:* "Rated PG-13 for language, some drug use, and brief sexuality." As part of his estranged father's estate, a sleazy salesman is instructed to give a sizable sum of money to a half-sister he didn't know about. He insinuates himself into her life, gets to know his young-teen nephew, but doesn't tell them the truth about who he is. The foul language is considerable, some of it from the young teenager; the drug use includes marijuana and a fair amount of drinking alcohol; and there is a lot of cigarette smoking. The brief sexuality most likely refers to a scene that has a woman unzipping a man's pants, but there is also sexual dialogue and the revealing clothing worn by a bartender.

★ *Rock of Ages:* "Rated PG-13 for sexual content, suggestive dancing, some heavy drinking, and language." Adapted from the Broadway hit, this rock musical set in the 1980s focuses on a young, naïve, small-town girl who wants to be a professional singer. Rather than chronicle all of the "sexual content" in this film, suffice it to say it is considerable, quite graphic, and though there is no nudity, there are costumes that are tight, short, or brief enough to leave little to the imagination, all of which prompted some critics to wonder in their reviews why this wasn't rated R. There are also a lot of scatological references, depicted and spoken of, including vomiting and urinating. And there is a lot of foul language, including the f-word spoken once.

★ *Total Recall:* "Rated PG-13 for intense sequences of sci-fi violence and action, some sexual content, brief nudity, and language." I'm not sure what the difference is between "sci-fi violence" and "action" (or does it mean "sci-fi violence and sci-fi action"?), but there is certainly plenty of both in this remake of the 1990 Arnold Schwarzenegger vehicle, which was rated R. This version stars Colin Farrell and is virtually a non-stop chase movie with lots of murderous mayhem and a very high body count, along with the usual profanity (and yes, that includes the f-word once). Perhaps, the most surprising moment for a PG-13 movie is when a prostitute on the street approaches Farrell and propositions him while opening her blouse to reveal three breasts (a repeat of a moment from the first film).

★ *Hope Springs:* "Rated PG-13 for mature thematic content involving sexuality." This film was sold as a rollicking comedy from the theatrical previews and TV spots, but it's actually a serious melodrama about an older couple (Meryl Streep and Tommy Lee Jones) that has been married for 32 years but has not been intimate for some time, and they no longer share a bedroom. At her insistence they go for a week of intensive couples counseling with a

Christian Bale in Christopher Nolan's Batman Begins *(2005) —Warner Bros.*

celebrity therapist (Steve Carell) and the bulk of the film is replete with graphic sexual talk and attempts at intimacy, to include oral sex in a public place. Obviously, from that description, this is very adult material and should be way out of bounds for anyone who is underage. This is another film that would seem to be an obvious candidate for the R rating.

Here are some further examples of ratings explanations from movies past, some with descriptive terms that seem vague if not off base, such as those for the recent *Batman* trilogy:

- *The Dark Knight Rises* (2012): "Rated PG-13 for intense sequences of violence and action, some sensuality, and language." No argument with "intense" or "violence and action." The phrase "some sensuality" apparently refers to a passionate embrace followed by the couple in bed together the next morning, suggesting they had sex the night before. And the "language" refers to several words that are considered among the "softer" swear words, the kind used commonly on network-television programs.

- *The Dark Knight* (2008): "Rated PG-13 for intense sequences of violence and some menace." In this case, instead of "violence and action," there's "violence and menace." It's a fine point, but is *The Dark Knight Rises* any less "menacing" than this one, and does this one have less "action" than *Rises*? The only allusion to sex in this film is when a character bursts into an office door and finds a man and woman buttoning up their clothing, which implies they've been having sex, but it goes by so fast that it apparently doesn't warrant a mention in the rating description. Profanities are used in about the same measure as *The Dark Knight Rises*, but notice that the rating description this time doesn't mention it.

★ *Batman Begins* (2005): "Rated PG-13 for intense action violence, disturbing images, and some thematic elements." The phrase "disturbing images" is interesting in this context, since "disturbing" was probably used in more reviews of *The Dark Knight* than any PG-13 film in recent memory. In this film, it may refer to Batman's origin story, which includes his being a child when he witnesses his parents being shot and killed. "Thematic elements" could mean anything, and could easily be applied to the two follow-up movies in this series—and maybe every movie that receives a rating. Also, this film has about the same level of profanity, but again, it's not mentioned in the description.

The earlier quartet of Batman movies from the late 1980s and '90s were also dark, though, arguably, not quite as dark as the more recent films. The first of those, *Batman* (1989), came out before descriptions were in use. The second, *Batman Returns* (1992), is considered by most people to be the darkest of this series, and it is "Rated PG-13 for brooding, dark violence." It was followed by *Batman Forever* (1995), "Rated PG-13 for strong stylized action," and finally, *Batman & Robin* (1997), "Rated PG-13 for strong stylized action and some innuendo."

It's interesting that the final two sequels' ratings single out "strong stylized action," since "stylized" applies to all of the Batman movies, including the most recent three. But replacing "violence" with "action" seems to water down the effect of these very violent films. And finally, the word "innuendo" for *Batman & Robin* seems odd since all four of the early Batman movies have a fair amount of sexual innuendo and double-entendres, but none of the earlier films' descriptions make mention of it. It may be that the board took particular notice of the rubber outfits worn by Batman, Robin, and Batgirl since, for the first time, they are anatomically suggestive and include nipples.

★ *Diary of a Wimpy Kid: Dog Days* (2012): "Rated PG for some rude humor." The previous two *Diary* movies had similar rating explanations: *Diary of a Wimpy Kid* (2010), "Rated PG for some rude humor and language," and *Diary of a Wimpy Kid: Rodrick Rules* (2011), "Rated PG for some mild, rude humor and mischief." These films are based on popular youth novels and aimed at youngsters, of course, with children's curiosity and tendency toward mischief leading the humor. The older brother has a dirty magazine in his bedroom, there are comments about girls, jokes about boogers, and juvenile name-calling, and in the first film, the younger brother accidentally urinates on his older brother. Still, the phrase "rude humor" is very vague for all of this. (When the comedy gets raunchier for an adult film, the board often switches from "rude humor" to "crude humor.")

★ *Trainspotting* (1996): "Rated R for graphic heroin use and resulting depravity, strong language, sex, nudity, and some violence." This is an example of a very specific rating description. And "depravity" isn't a word you'll see often, though it certainly would apply to a lot of movies.

★ *The Client* (1994): "Rated PG-13 for a child in jeopardy and brief language." Here's another example of specificity since the entire film is about "a child in jeopardy." But the phrase "brief language" is troubling, as there is quite a bit of profanity in this film, by adults and pre-teen children. In addition, an adult, and later a child, use a familiar obscene hand gesture. There are also pre-teens smoking. What's more, there's a fair amount of violence, though it's either off camera or threatening in nature. The film opens with a man attempting suicide by asphyxiation, he then puts a gun in the face of a young boy, and a few moments later puts the gun in his own mouth—but as he pulls the trigger, the camera quickly shifts to the faces of two boys who are watching. Also, a boy is threatened with a knife and later chased through a hospital. It may be that the rating board simply feels that all of these moments, along with other gunplay and mayhem, fall under the purview of "jeopardy." I'm not sure many parents would make that leap.

★ *Hannibal* (2001): "Rated R for strong gruesome violence, some nudity, and language." This sequel to *The Silence of the Lambs* (1991, just before rating descriptions were put into effect) is indeed "gruesome," a term that applies equally to all of the Hannibal Lecter films. But for some reason the word "grisly" is substituted for "gruesome" in rating descriptions for the sequels/prequels: *Red Dragon* (2002), "Rated R for violence, grisly images, language, some nudity and sexuality" and *Hannibal Rising* (2007), "Rated R for strong grisly violent content and some language/sexual references."

The following rating descriptions just seem odd, some in an amusing way, many more in a puzzling way, and sometimes in a manner that seems to be commenting on the film with an opinion— almost a review instead of a neutral description:

★ *Twister* (1996): "Rated PG-13 for intense depiction of very bad weather." Maybe weathercasters on news programs should give ratings to the weather: "Yes, Shelley, it's going to be a PG-13 week of bad weather."

★ *The Day after Tomorrow* (2004): "Rated PG-13 for intense situations of peril." In this end-of-the-world yarn, the "peril" is caused by "very bad weather," though the board chose to leave that phrase out this time.

★ *2012* (2009): "Rated PG-13 for intense disaster sequences and some language." Another apocalyptic weather yarn, this one gets right to the nut, since all of these movies are part of the "disaster" genre.

★ *Alice in Wonderland* (2010): "Rated PG for fantasy action/violence involving scary images and situations, and for a smoking caterpillar." Uh, oh. The 1951 Disney cartoon version also has that smoking caterpillar, but it was made before ratings, and then in 1971 for a reissue it was rated G.

★ *The Indian in the Cupboard* (1995): "Rated PG for mild language and brief video images of violence and sexy dancing." Suggestive dancing is not uncommon in a lot of movies, but this is the only time I've seen it singled out as a reason for a rating.

★ *Alien vs. Predator* (2004): "Rated PG-13 for violence, language, horror images, slime, and gore." This is the only rating description I know of that singles out "slime" as a reason for a rating. (Perhaps, it would have been applied to *Ghostbusters* if that film weren't made well before rating descriptions.)

★ *Natural Born Killers* (1994): "Rated R for extreme violence and graphic carnage, for shocking images, and for strong language and sexuality." This one specifies "graphic carnage" and "shocking images," the latter in particular seeming to be a biased, but not inaccurate, comment.

- ★ *Team America World Police* (2004): "Rated R for graphic, crude, and sexual humor, violent images and strong language—all involving puppets." Here's another long description and the comment at the end, perhaps serves as a warning to parents that, despite being enacted entirely by puppets, this is not a children's movie.

- ★ *Jefferson in Paris* (1995): "Rated PG-13 for mature theme, some images of violence, and a bawdy puppet show." The phrase "mature theme" is a common one in ratings descriptions, but then this one gets quite specific regarding the puppet-show sequence, without which this might easily be a PG movie.

- ★ *Public Enemies* (2009): "Rated R for gangster violence and some language." Some rating descriptions add the film's genre or some other plot-descriptive term as a modifier, although any time a person is killed or maimed or hurt in some violent manner, it's the same kind of violence, more or less. But for this mob movie, instead of simply "violence," it's "gangster violence"—as opposed to:

- ★ *Tombstone* (1993), which is "Rated R for strong western violence."

- ★ *Shaun of the Dead* (2003), "Rated R for zombie violence. "

- ★ *Predators* (2010), "Rated R for strong creature violence" (Look out for those strong creatures.)

- ★ *Prometheus* (2012), "Rated R for sci-fi violence."

- ★ *Freddy Got Fingered* (2001): "Rated R for crude sexual and bizarre humor, and for strong language." Actually, "bizarre humor" could apply to a lot of movies—perhaps everything by the Coen Brothers or Tim Burton—but it's unusual to see the label in the rating box.

★ *Charlie and the Chocolate Factory* (2005): "Rated PG for quirky situations, action, and mild language." Similarly, referring to the film's "situations" as "quirky" actually parrots a lot of real movie reviews of Tim Burton's work. But in this case, considering how dark it is for a children's film, I wouldn't find the word "disturbing" out of place.

★ *My Fellow Americans* (1996): "Rated PG-13 for salty language and innuendo." The antiquated phrase "salty lan-

Simon Pegg amongst the zombies in Shaun of the Dead *(2004) —Universal*

guage" seems an odd choice for a movie description, and "innuendo" isn't used very often either.

★ *Naked Gun 33 1/3: The Final Insult* (1994): "Rated PG-13 for off-color humor." Today, the word "crude" seems to have replaced "off-color."

★ *Dumb & Dumber* (1994): "Rated PG-13 for off-color humor." Apparently, that was the in phrase for 1994.

★ *Police Academy: Mission to Moscow* (1994, No. 7 in the series): "Rated PG for comic sensuality." Apparently, sex jokes played for laughs are OK for kids, including, as seen in this film, topless women partially underwater.

★ *The Fugitive* (1993): "Rated PG-13 for a murder and other action sequences in an adventure setting." In this case, a man is shot and killed at point-blank range and a woman is brutally beaten to death in her own home—so how does "an adventure setting" qualify that? Perhaps, it's the "Indiana Jones" rule, further justified by the presence of Harrison Ford in this film.

★ *Mother's Boys* (1994): "Rated R for language and for a mother's sociopathic behavior." This description has a psychoanalytical approach we don't see very often . . . but it's not wrong.

★ *Dead Alive* (1992): "Rated R for an abundance of outrageous gore." This is a gruesome zombie comedy, and perhaps, the "comedy" part explains the use of "outrageous," though it still sounds like an opinion. Other zombie movies in the same ballpark have R ratings described as "strong violence and gore" (*28 Days Later*, 2002), "pervasive strong horror violence and gore" (*Dawn of the Dead*,

2004), "pervasive strong violence and gore" (*Land of the Dead*, 2005), "strong violence and gore" (*28 Weeks Later*), "horror violence/gore" (*Zombieland*, 2009), along with the usual warnings about sex, nudity, language, etc.

★ *Se7en* (1995): "Rated R for grisly afterviews of horrific and bizarre killings, and for strong language." The word "bizarre" seems to connote an opinion, but this one must have been a challenge for board members since they also invented a word to describe it. The film doesn't have much violence, as such, but there are stomach-churning moments after detectives stumble on victims of a serial killer. Perhaps "grisly" or "disturbing" would have been applicable, but "afterviews"? Really?

★ *The Cell* (2000): "Rated R for bizarre violence and sexual images, nudity, and language." Here's "bizarre" again, and though this was an odd movie, whenever the board chooses to use the word "bizarre" it sounds like they're reviewing rather than rating.

★ *Project X* (2012): "Rated R for crude and sexual content throughout, nudity, drugs, drinking, pervasive language, reckless behavior, and mayhem—all involving teens." Aside from holding what may be the record for the longest description ever, this one is a bit more specific and adds the tagline that it all of this material involves underage kids, a warning that is becoming more and more common as raunchy humor overwhelms not just the majority of comedies being released, but also a preponderance of movies about teenagers—which, by implication, would also seem to be targeting them as an audience, despite the R rating.

- ★ *Kick-Ass* (2010): "Rated R for strong brutal violence throughout, pervasive language, sexual content, nudity, and some drug use—some involving children." Maybe another reason for the rating should be the film's title.

Chapter 8 FILMMAKERS AND STUDIOS

What in the World Are They Thinking?

One morning in late July of 1989, after I'd been a movie critic for a little over a decade, the office mail delivered four tickets to a movie preview instead of the usual two, along with a letter that encouraged me to bring my kids to this new family picture that was opening in the next couple of weeks. The preview was a radio-sponsored giveaway, a free evening screening that would be packed with the radio station's fans, and they were guaranteed to be rowdy, laughing at anything and everything. You might think that by this time I'd be savvy enough to know better than to accept such an invitation on face value before any specific information about the film has gone public. But no, I confess to being just as naïve as the next guy.

The movie was *Parenthood*, of which the current TV series is a spinoff. The film, directed by Ron Howard and starring Steve Martin, with a cast of familiar comic actors in support, seemed a perfect fit for my wife Joyce and I. We were married the year before, a second marriage for both of us, and we each brought several children into the mix of our rather large blended family. And when these tickets arrived, they were for a movie we had seen advertised relentlessly on TV as a sort of Disney-style family farce, with a tagline explaining that it was a "comedy about life, love, and the gentle art of raising children."

So we thought about which of our kids we should take. We settled on one of Joyce's daughters and her new husband, newlyweds anxious to start a family, and this seemed like a good way to show them some of the comic misadventures ahead. Although we did have in the back of our minds an unanswered question: Why is *Parenthood* rated PG-13 instead of PG?

When the time arrived and the four of us settled in to watch the film, it unspooled as something more than the light comedy we expected. "Comedy-drama," or "dramatic comedy," might have better described this ensemble film about a family of five, with Steve Martin and Mary Steenburgen as the parents of three young children—and their extended family, to include Martin's sister (Dianne Wiest), a divorcee with a troubled son (Leaf Phoenix) and a teenage daughter (Martha Plimpton) who, unbeknownst to Mom, lets her boyfriend (Keanu Reeves) sleep over in her bedroom; Martin's brother (Tom Hulce), a drifter/con-artist who owes money to the mob and who dumps his illegitimate son on his aging parents; Martin's other sister (Harley Jane Kozak), her overzealous husband (Rick Moranis) and the daughter he won't let be a child; and the patriarch of the group (Jason Robards), who was the kind of father Martin has vowed not to be.

All of which is fine, but we were seriously shocked by how raunchy the film proved to be, and with Joyce's young, newly married daughter and son-in-law sitting next to us, we winced at every sleazy joke and casual sexual reference, which covered the gamut in conversation or by visual demonstration, from teen sex and teen pregnancy to oral sex in a car (referred to as "oral highway") to masturbation to a sight gag with a vibrator to a teen's stash of pornography to a discussion of possible abortion and plenty of foul language along the way. And, of course, a few gross-out bodily function gags.

Afterward, it certainly stimulated discussion among us, and we overheard a number of other people as they left the theater talking about how, if this is Hollywood's idea of a family film, well, that explains a lot.

To my mind, *Parenthood* is the perfect example of a movie that would have been just as good, maybe better, without all the raunchy material. Obviously, the studio decided to sell the film as something much less raunchy than it was—deceptive, but not atypical advertising—and as the film rolled out in early August of 1989, I heard from a lot of people who were shocked by some of the things they saw in this so-called "family comedy."

But all of this also speaks to the changing times over the next twenty-plus years. Today, a movie like *Parenthood*, instead of being

Young Kevin (Jasen Fisher) has a heart-to-heart chat with his dad (Steve Martin) in Ron Howard's Parenthood ***(1989) —Universal***

advertised in a misleading way with TV clips avoiding the naughtier sex jokes, would instead put those gags front and center in the advertising. The dirtiest jokes would be selling points. And let's face it, nearly every modern prime-time TV sitcom is probably worse every single week, so the thinking is, hey, kids see it all the time anyway, what difference does it make?

And though *Parenthood* is now more than two decades old, it remains a best-selling DVD, so people are obviously buying/renting it today, and I wonder if a new generation of parents feels the same way about it all these years later as I did on that evening in 1989. Perhaps people who saw it in the '80s and forgot everything except that it made them laugh are looking at it again with fresh eyes now that they have kids of their own and asking, how in the world did that movie get away with a PG-13 instead of an R?

Although content has changed in the sense that a lot more offensive material is allowed in broad-based films than used to be, Hollywood's approach to selling these films has not changed much. *Parenthood* was pitched to audiences as a flat-out comedy despite its considerable dramatic content because the studio feared that if audiences knew ahead of time that the film was really more of a sober drama laced with comedic moments, they might not come. At least not in the droves that ultimately made *Parenthood* such a hit.

The same thing happened in the summer of 2012 with *Hope Springs*, starring Meryl Streep and Tommy Lee Jones as a long-married couple trying to reignite their sex life. The trailers and TV spots pitched it as a laugh-a-minute comedy (hey, Steve Carell's their therapist!), but it's really a very dramatic film punctuated by a few comic moments, all of them in the trailer. And it's another PG-13 movie that's way too adult for teens. But this time the approach backfired and *Hope Springs* was a box-office disappointment.

Then there's the 2012 independent film *Moonrise Kingdom*, "Rated PG-13 for sexual content and smoking," an offbeat comedy-drama set in 1960's New England about a pair of 12-year-olds (Kara Hayward, Jared Gilman) who run away together. The "sexual content" referred to in the rating is mostly verbal between the children as they hug while in their underwear, but they also French kiss, he puts his hand on her chest and she comments on his erection (which is not shown).

There is also a subplot about an adulterous affair between the girl's mother (Frances McDormand) and the local police chief (Bruce Willis), which is discussed but not demonstrated; there is brief nudity as a topless McDormand washes her hair in a sink (shown very briefly under the opening credits); a fair amount of profanity; and a pre-teen smokes and drinks a beer. Smoking among adults is authentic to the era, of course, and some characters frequently light up.

Granted, *Moonrise Kingdom*, as a low-budget independent film was never going to attain the same level of popularity as *Parenthood*, and, in fact, had a gradual release, primarily on the art-house circuit as opposed to opening in 3,000 theaters on its first day. But when movies are rated, no one knows how they will go over with audiences, and this is another one that is obviously not for kids. So why then is it rated PG-13?

What's wrong with these pictures being rated R, which would automatically indicate that some of the content should be out of reach for young children? Sometimes when I see these films I wonder what in the world CARA, or for that matter, the filmmakers, were thinking.

In 1992, a film called *Radio Flyer*, which was "Rated PG-13 for theme (child abuse) and violence," was being advertised on TV as a feel-good *E.T.*-style fantasy about two young brothers building a flying machine from their Radio Flyer wagon. What was not shown in those ads was the child abuse of the rating description, and as such, it was yet another falsely advertised movie that was very much not for children.

The film begins with a father (unbilled Tom Hanks) whose children are bickering, so he decides to tell them the story of his own childhood, as we see his younger self (now played by Elijah Wood) and his little brother (Joseph Mazzello) living with their mother (Lorraine Bracco) and stepfather (Adam Baldwin). The stepfather brutally abuses the youngest boy, so his older brother tries to protect him, eventually coming up with the plan to build a sort of makeshift helicopter to fly the boy away to freedom.

The film is much debated among fans as to whether it should be taken literally or metaphorically, although there are some clear fantasy elements, and critics are sharply divided, but generally negative about its worth. But any way you slice it, this is not a film kids should see. The abuse sequences are quite scary as the stepfather's face is veiled so that he's a kind of monster image, the monster in the closet, the monster under the bed.

On the other end of the spectrum is the 1993 film *The Good Son*, a rare example of a rating that got it right, but for the wrong reason. The film was an attempt to expand, or perhaps, change the image of child actor Macaulay Culkin, who had become a huge star with the first two *Home Alone* holiday comedies. In *The Good Son*, Culkin is akin to Patty McCormick's character in *The Bad Seed*, an evil-spirited child who reels in his cousin (Elijah Wood) for pranks and mischief that escalate from breaking windows to killing animals to causing a ten-car pileup with a man-size dummy. When Wood tries to step away from all this destructive activity, Culkin begins to use him as a patsy for his crimes.

The Good Son is "Rated R for acts of violence and terror involving a disturbed child." But in the strictest terms of content, there is really nothing in the film that goes beyond or even rises up to what we often see in other PG or PG-13 films. The violence is off-screen and, aside from a few scattered profanities—including Culkin's calculated use of the f-word—there is nothing here that would ordinarily merit an R rating. Except that it's Macaulay Culkin.

At the time Culkin was the 1990s equivalent of Shirley Temple, and it was thought it would be disturbing to children to see him as an unfeeling underage monster. Just seeing Culkin's face in a TV ad or on a poster would be enough to entice children, so this must be the reason for the harsher rating, or so the thinking went in 1993, but, again, it's just speculation because CARA would never say one way or the other. Certainly, the rating is justified, as it should be for any movie that is so obviously out of bounds for children, but it is, nonetheless, an anomaly.

Culkin's two blockbusters, *Home Alone* (1990) and *Home Alone 2: Lost in New York* (1992), both set during the holidays and both rated PG, are violent comedies, but that didn't keep any kids away. Both films were embraced by family audiences and both shot up to the top of the box-office tallies for their respective years (*Home Alone* was 1990's No. 1 movie; *Home Alone 2* was 1992's second biggest film, after Disney's *Aladdin.*) There was also a PG-rated *Home Alone 3* in 1997, but without Culkin or any other original cast members, and the film belly-flopped, coming in at No. 67 for that year.

But another young child's mischief making in a 1990 PG-rated movie was much more troubling. *Problem Child*, a sort of zany spoof of *The Bad Seed*, is about an evil child (Michael Oliver) adopted by a hapless nice guy (John Ritter) and his social-climbing wife (Amy Yasbeck), and the film is replete with tasteless gags about child abandonment, adoption, and serial killers, among other touchy subjects (including those old standbys, flatulence and urinating). But the film was a surprise hit at the box office, so, naturally, *Problem Child 2* arrived the next year (with the original cast intact), this one rated PG-13 and seemingly determined to outdo its predecessor in terms of gross-out material. It effortlessly achieves that goal. The sequel even has a sex scene! And again, both were sold directly and unashamedly to small fry.

These films and many others make you wonder why movies aimed at youngsters, sold to youngsters, and, perhaps, even created with youngsters in mind, contain so much inappropriate material. Don't these filmmakers have children? When a story is proposed or a script is pitched, doesn't anyone sitting around the table express misgivings about vulgar jokes or the level of violence or sexual material in movies aimed at young people?

For that matter, does anyone on the CARA board ever say, hey, these adult movies with sexual themes or violence aren't really for kids, maybe an R rating isn't so off the mark? Instead it seems that filmmakers simply want to get away with as much as they can, as if it's some sort of competition to sneak in as much questionable material as possible, regardless of the nature of the film. And the film raters tacitly agree to help them out.

The 1984 release, *The Buddy System,* is an old-fashioned, romantic comedy starring Richard Dreyfuss and Susan Sarandon, but it is also a film of its era, and definitely not the family film it was touted to be in its marketing. In my original review I wrote that "It is Hollywood's naive, generalized view that men and women always go to bed together on the first date, that businessmen have sex-filled lunch hours with their secretaries, and that all children—no matter how young—swear like sailors, even if the adults around them don't." It was rated PG before the PG-13 came onboard.

The Buddy System, naturally, took its rating and went to the box office happy. But sometimes movies that get PG ratings want PG-13s, and sometimes those that get PG-13s want PGs.

Sylvester Stallone apparently wanted his 1992 comedy *Stop! Or My Mom Will Shoot* to be rated PG-13. The film is about an unmarried veteran L.A. cop (Stallone) whose wacky mother (Estelle Getty) visits from New Jersey and drives him crazy, eventually ingratiating herself into his work by witnessing a murder. Despite considerable violence and mayhem, some profanity and a few vulgarisms, the film was given a PG rating. But that wasn't strong enough for the filmmakers, so they inserted a scene that has Stallone in the shower, revealing his backside, and they resubmitted the film to the rating board and it was re-rated to PG-13.

And the family film *My Girl* (1991) was originally rated PG-13, apparently for the death of a sympathetic child character toward the end—and, perhaps, because that child was played by Macaulay Culkin, yes that cute kid from the *Home Alone* movies again. The film also has also quite a bit of swearing and in many ways is about death, with the title character (Anna Chlumsky) obsessing over the passing of her mother, and her father (Dan Aykroyd) being a mortician. Upon appeal, the film was re-rated PG without any changes. The sequel, *My Girl 2* (1994), earned a PG automatically, despite a moment of marijuana smoking.

One of the things that bothers me most about the preponderance of raunchy humor in movies is that so much of it is the same thing over and over again, without any wit or cleverness in evidence. It's lazy and displays a certain contempt for the audience. Where's the effectiveness or even the shock value of doing some kind of vulgar joke if every other film does the same gag, or a variation on the same gag?

In 1974, Mel Brooks introduced flatulence to mainstream movies with *Blazing Saddles* in a famous scene that has the cowboys sitting around a campfire, eating beans and cutting loose, a sequence that seems to go on forever, which only adds to the silliness. Sometime later, during an appearance on *The Tonight Show With Johnny Carson*, Brooks said something to the effect that he's proud that he'll be remembered as the man who introduced the fart to movies. He was joking, of course, and the audience howled. But that's exactly what he did, and it's another example of opening a door that was previously closed.

What was in 1974 merely a movie moment of surprise and nervous laughter began a ripple effect that is still going on today. How many films, mainly comedies, have a joke in that same vein—from the sleaziest, most vulgar adult pictures to the most innocent children's movies? Dozens, or more likely, hundreds of films released since 1974 feature variations on that gag and many more still show up in new movies every year. Audiences still titter, so those jokes won't be going away any time soon, but to me it's more than worn out its welcome. What was unique is 1974 is now stale and overused.

Movie moments like this are often played for shock value the first time, to earn an embarrassed laugh or to startle an audience, but then other filmmakers copy it to death. The first time I saw a movie that showed someone sitting on a toilet, rather than just going into a stall or bathroom and shutting the door, was in *Catch-22* (1970), an R-rated film. It was a shock moment in 1970, but now it's a common sight in many movies, most recently the title youngster in the PG-rated *Diary of a Wimpy Kid: Dog Days* (2012). But the grossest follow-up is arguably Jeff Daniels bouncing around on a toilet for a lengthy, noisy gag in *Dumb & Dumber* (1994), rated PG-13.

The first time I saw someone graphically vomiting, rather than merely running to the bathroom and hacking off-camera, was in the R-rated *An Unmarried Woman* (1978), as the central character, Erica (Jill Clayburgh), is chatting with her husband (Michael Murphy) while they walk on a busy street. She notices that he's upset and he tearfully tells her that he's in love with another woman and is leaving her, at which point Erica goes into an alley and throws up in a trashcan. And ever since, vomiting has been graphically displayed in movies over and over, often with babies or children projectile vomiting in someone's face as a gag in many PG and PG-13 movies. This joke reached some kind of zenith (or nadir) in the R-rated *Monty Python's The Meaning of Life* (1983), in a gross-out sequence that goes on forever.

Similarly, the first time I heard the f-word in a movie was the R-rated *MASH* (1970), the anti-war film set in Korea, but actually meant to resonate with the then-raging Vietnam War. The word is spoken once during a football game, but that's all it took to open the door. Many R-rated movies subsequently began using the word, but it wasn't until the 1980s that it began to be used over and over again, to lessening impact in my mind since its use constantly is not just as an expletive, but also as an adjective, modifier, preposition, adverb.

In the early '80s, I used to refer to it as the "Eddie Murphy Word," since he used it in every other sentence and all kinds of combinations in the *48 HRS.* and *Beverly Hills Cop* films.

In the late '80s, it became the "Bruce Willis Word," thanks to the *Die Hard* movies and others of his action pictures. And in the '90s, it was the "Quentin Tarantino Word" and the "Martin Scorsese Word," since their films seemed to use it more than any others—although, it's also common in the movies of many other stars and filmmakers.

But to what effect? When it's heard so incessantly on a film's soundtrack, the shock value quickly wears off and it merely becomes redundant and annoying. By one count, the f-word is used in Scorsese's *Goodfellas* (1990) two hundred and ninety-six times, which seems excessive even by Hollywood standards.

One brief sequence that uses the expletive over and over was responsible for the R rating received by *Four Weddings and a Funeral.* The opening scene of this very light, frothy comedy uses the f-word in what may be a record number of variations in a very brief period as Hugh Grant wakes up, realizes he is late for an important appointment, and mutters a variety of comic phrases under his breath as he leaps out of bed and races to get dressed.

Before it had received its rating, *Four Weddings and a Funeral* was the opening-night film of the 1994 Sundance Film Festival with screenings in three auditoriums of a Salt Lake City multiplex. It was described in the festival catalog as "a stylish and witty romantic comedy," with "rare . . . intelligence and heart." It didn't mention the foul

Slim Pickens and Alex Karras at the conclusion of the most famous scene in Mel Brooks' Blazing Saddles *(1974) —Warner Bros.*

language, of course. After celebrity introductions in each auditorium, with Grant and his co-star Andie MacDowell in attendance, the lights went down, the movie started and that opening moment so shocked audience members that a surprising number of invited guests, including Utah legislators, walked out in the first five minutes.

Remember that scene in *A Christmas Story* (1983) when little Ralphie utters a cuss word (which the audience hears as "fudge"), and the narrator (Ralphie as an adult) explains: "Only I didn't say 'fudge.' I said THE word, the big one, the queen-mother of dirty words, the 'f-dash-dash-dash' word!"

It was a clever, amusing and effective way of dealing with that situation without resorting to actually saying the word, just as the father's profanity in the film was a garbled slur of incomprehensible mumbling. Everyone knew what was being said, except maybe children in the audience—and they didn't need to know. But it was put over inoffensively.

In a way, that was a real throwback to the way movies were made during the Production Code era, when subtlety ruled. And it reminded me of the 1957 Glenn Ford military comedy *Don't Go Near the Water*, in which a sailor uses profanity constantly. But every time he does, a sort of foghorn noise drowns him out.

The way *A Christmas Story* dealt with this situation may seem quaint to modern audiences—heck, it seemed quaint in 1983—since we are used to hearing every cuss word, every vulgar phrase, and seeing everything spelled out rather than hinted at in every movie and TV show we see. But in my book, it's better than being insulted and offended and verbally assaulted every time you take in some performance entertainment.

Today, the use of that most dreaded of cuss words casts a much wider net, being used once (at least) in nearly every PG-13 movie—so much that it's lost its punch. Overuse undercuts any intention by the filmmakers for the word to make some sort of point. It seems like a contest between filmmakers to see how many times they can sneak it into a PG-13 movie, and it's invariably overused in R-rated films.

The f-word has become a cliche, a crutch to prop up weak writing.

But filmmakers continue to be quite proud of its usage—especially when it's thrown into a movie aimed at younger audiences, as if that will somehow make the film more appealing to an older crowd. As an extreme example of this misplaced loyalty, two DVDs that I know of deliberately revel in the use of that word with featurettes that count out in a jokey fashion the number of times the expletive is used, *Scarface* (1983) and *Lock, Stock and Two Smoking Barrels* (1998).

Another lesson lost on Hollywood is that less is more, and this is never truer than with violence in movies. Everything on the big screen is literal and can be overwhelming, and one of the reasons is because it's so big. Movies are forty feet high, in amplified stereo, with slow-motion mayhem and dizzying edits, and, of course, digital enhancement as vehicles crash, high-rises collapse, and bullets tear at human flesh (or, in the case of the superheroes that are so prevalent in movies today, bounce off).

Recently, while watching an old '50's crime film on TV, I couldn't help but notice that when someone was shot with several bullets and fell to the ground, there were no visible wounds and no blood. And a few nights later I noticed that in an old 1970's film that did show blood, it was so vividly red and thick that it appeared to be paint. Compare that to all the violent action thrillers and comic-book movies in theaters these days, where the havoc is so graphic and over-the-top that it's often rather disgusting . . . and yet it is no more realistic.

Just because modern movies show blood and open wounds and all kinds of carnage, just because we see bullet holes and a lot of splatter, doesn't make it any more real. Hyper reality is as phony as restrained reality. And many of these films treat the violence lightly, even frivolously, and in some cases as if it just doesn't matter. Often an enormous amount of death or injury isn't even commented upon.

Take the 2008 fantasy thriller *Wanted*, starring James McAvoy and Angelina Jolie. There's a scene where the film's hero boards a train that is packed with passengers, and a subsequent fight leads to the train falling into a canyon. The protagonist survives, but nothing is ever mentioned about the massive number of people on the train whose lives are obviously lost in the crash.

Now add to *Wanted* all the buildings and vehicles that contain human beings and are crushed, smashed, blown up, and otherwise destroyed in disaster movies, superhero pictures, and other action films, ranging from the *Dark Knight* trilogy to the *Iron Man* franchise to *Transformers* and its sequels, and there is an amazing amount of implied carnage on the screen.

Remember the nuclear explosion in *Indiana Jones and the Kingdom of the Crystal Skull* (2008)? There was never any mention of the fallout from that test (which is played for laughs). Apparently, the value of human life in our video game/comic book culture isn't worth much.

Of course, you may say that all of this violence is meant to provide thrilling action, and that we're not supposed to be distracted by nearly invisible collateral damage. And besides, it's only a movie!

Well, it's hard to argue with that. And I'll admit that I have enjoyed a lot of these movies as much as anyone, but I worry about children being exposed to this kind of thing, especially when there's so much real-life violence brought home to us via TV and the Internet. Maybe I'm having second thoughts about destruction as entertainment.

In *Superman Returns* (2006), the Man of Steel was racing around Manhattan (OK, Metropolis, Gotham City, whatever), rescuing people as high-rise buildings started to tremble and falling objects threatened people on the ground. But now, just a few years later, our superheroes seem to be saving mankind by killing off half of the city's workforce, the result of concrete-and-steel towers being destroyed in the name of "saving the city."

Maybe in 2013, when Superman returns again in *Man of Steel*, he'll set the other guys straight. Or, maybe he'll go to the dark side along with Batman and the Avengers, et al. (As of this writing *Man of Steel* has not yet opened, but is scheduled for June 2013.)

Adults do care about movie ratings, and not just for their kids. Many use them for themselves, something that was proven to me over and over during my years on the movie beat. Whenever a high-profile action film was on the horizon, I'd start getting calls asking what it was going to be rated.

There was a lot of disappointment when *Patriot Games* (1992) was given an R rating, since the first film in the Jack Ryan franchise, *The Hunt for Red October* (1990), carried a PG. I can't say I was surprised when the third and fourth films in the series, *Clear and Present Danger* (1994) and *The Sum of All Fears* (2002), were rated PG-13.

Ditto *The Fugitive* (1993), which began showing TV ads that psyched up the audience before the film was rated, with the narrator saying in rapid-fire trailer-speak: "This film has not yet been rated." Same with the first *Mission: Impossible* (1996).

But don't think it's just men and action movies. I had calls from quite a few female moviegoers who were fans of the book *The Bridges of Madison County* when that movie was about to come out in 1995, wondering if it would be a steamy R-rated film or toned down enough for book clubs to attend together without being embarrassed. Initially, the film did get an R, but after an appeal, *Bridges* managed to squeak by with a PG-13.

In these days of the raunchy *Bridesmaids* attracting a largely female audience, it may seem odd to think that people cared about what a rating might be in 1995, but many adults still care. Not everyone wants to be exposed to *Bridesmaids*-level sleaze. And if Hollywood filmmakers and studio chiefs didn't recognize this, they wouldn't be pursuing PG-13 ratings for so many films.

R-rated blockbusters like *Bridesmaids* and *The Hangover* are still exceptions to the rule. But by its very label, the PG-13 would seem to suggest such recent films as *Crazy, Stupid, Love*, *The Lucky One*, *The Vow*, etc., are fine for a teen-inclusive audience.

On the basis of several rave reviews, and since it received a PG-13 rating, my wife and I made the mistake of seeing *Crazy, Stupid, Love* in 2011. The central sexual themes are bad enough, but not one of the many reviews I read pointed out the distressing subplot in this romantic comedy that has a thirteen-year-old boy (Jonah Bobo) fantasizing about his seventeen-year-old babysitter (Analeigh Tipton), who in turn has a crush on the boy's father (Steve Carell).

This underage girl takes nude photos of herself (nothing is shown, thankfully), develops prints, and puts them in an envelope with the name of Carell's character on it. Naturally, her parents find the photos

Things get complicated for Jonah Bobo and Analeigh Tipton in Crazy, Stupid, Love *(2011) —Warner Bros.*

and (sarcasm alert) "hilarious" misinterpretations ensue. But here's the kicker: At the end of the film, after everyone has supposedly learned a few lessons about life, love, and monogamy, the thirteen-year-old boy graduates from eighth grade and guess what the seventeen-year-old girl gives him as a gift. That's right. The nude photos! Is that really the kind of thing teenage moviegoers should be seeing?

In 1990, a PG-13 film that was aimed directly at a very young audience was the Arnold Schwarzenegger comedy *Kindergarten Cop*, another example of a film that was advertised on television with cutesy ad spots that made it appear to be about this oversized police officer interacting with children in humorous ways. And there are some very funny scenes with 5-year-olds. But the film is primarily about Schwarzenegger as an undercover L.A. cop masquerading as a kindergarten teacher to take down a villain by using the guy's young son as bait.

At the end of the film Schwarzenegger blows the bad guy away in front of the boy. There is also other violence, including wife abuse, and some language, and sexual innuendo. Yet, the studio had no compunctions about selling the film to kids and families as a happy comedy.

MORE PG/PG-13 FILMS FROM 1990 THAT PUSH THE LIMITS:

★ *Robin Hood: Prince of Thieves* : The villain attempts to rape his new bride moments after their wedding ceremony.

★ *Sweet Talker*: A con artist and his mentor go into his apartment where his landlady is waiting for him in his bed, nude under the sheets.

★ *Only the Lonely*: A cop spends the night with his girlfriend, then hides her when his mother comes home.

- ★ *Problem Child 2*: A videotape of a babysitter and her boyfriend having sex is shown on the side of a house at night for all the neighbors to see.

- ★ *Don't Tell Mom the Babysitter's Dead*: A teenage boy casually smokes marijuana with his buddies in his bedroom.

- ★ *Dutch*: A pre-teen boy sleeps in the back seat of a car with his head resting on a prostitute's chest as he drools on her.

- ★ *The Rocketeer*: The camera goes in for a closeup of the lead actress' low-cut cleavage while a comic character makes a vulgar remark.

- ★ *Drop Dead Fred*: an imaginary "playmate" slides on the floor, looks up a woman's dress and utters a vulgar comment.

The level of violence in *Kindgergarten Cop*, *Robin Hood*, and *The Rocketeer*, the continuous stream of vulgarity in *Drop Dead Fred* and *Problem Child 2* and casual drug abuse of *Don't Tell Mom* are typical examples of how jaded people who make movies had become by 1990. So imagine how much more jaded they are two decades-plus later.

Certainly, to some degree, audiences have also become jaded, but judging from the comments I frequently hear from parents, most are still disturbed by the kind of things their children are exposed to through the media—whether it's movies, television, videogames, music, magazines, even news reports. Without suggesting censorship, a little common sense or sensitivity on the part of Hollywood movers and shakers couldn't hurt.

Once upon a time, long, long ago, Hollywood seemed to know how to make movies for adults and movies for children—and sometimes movies that appealed to both adults and children. But today, movies are more often not suitable for either.

If the moviegoers I hear from are any indication, even the box-office successes that include such material more often than not have sent audience members out of the theater feeling they enjoyed the film in spite of those elements not because of them. But I think it's more than just the syndrome of cynical movies-by-committee. I think it's because these filmmakers have lost touch with, for lack of a better term, Middle America.

Hollywood likes to think of itself as enlightened and smarter, hipper and more correct than anyone else in the room. And by Hollywood, I mean, of course, studio chiefs, producers, filmmakers, and movie stars. Most of them once lived outside Los Angeles or Manhattan, co-existing with ordinary people on a day-to-day basis —until they became successful. Then they radically changed their lifestyles to include chic dining spots, expensive parties, mingling with "beautiful people," and, often, drugs.

During my interview with Steven Spielberg lo those many years ago, I told him that it was an interesting idea to take the haunted house out of a remote setting and put it in modern-day suburbia in *Poltergeist*. But I added that the film had one scene that threw me, when the parents giggle as they sneak a marijuana cigarette in their bedroom.

I confessed to him that I had had a few friends who had experimented with pot when they were young in the wild and woolly 1960s, but once they got married, had kids and settled into careers and suburban life, they never thought about it again and certainly didn't want their kids using drugs as a guilty pleasure, like the parents in *Poltergeist*.

With a straight face, Spielberg told me he was surprised to hear that because, as he put it, all of his friends smoked marijuana.

Of course, that was more than 30 years ago when he was in his mid-30s and had not yet married and had children, but it's still safe to say that Steven Spielberg travels in very different social circles than the rest of us.

Movies during the so-called Golden Age of Cinema often extolled courage and goodness, perhaps best exemplified by Frank Capra's comic stories of nobility among men and women who were striving to do the right thing in the midst of conflict, frustration, or corruption: *It Happened One Night* (1934), *Mr. Deeds Goes to Town* (1936), *Mr. Smith Goes to Washington* (1939), *Meet John Doe* (1941), and many others were a remarkable string of optimistic overcoming-all-odds pictures that lifted audiences and encouraged them to leave the theater and become better people. And Capra occasionally employed fantasy elements with the same result, as in *Lost Horizon* (1937) and *It's a Wonderful Life* (1946).

Many of these were enormously popular Oscar-contenders and all are now recognized as classics and have been revived with regularity over the ensuing decades. In those years, there were still plenty of dark, cynical, and fantastic movies being shown in theaters, but Hollywood seemed to be able to balance them equally with human stories that were more confident in the human spirit, standing up for courage and goodness among everyday people. But today, the dark, cynical, outside-the-real-world pictures seem to dominate. And they are often populated with characters you'd rather avoid than embrace.

Take, for example, some of the biggest hits of 2012: superheroes battling to save the Earth from evils outside human control (*The Avengers, The Dark Knight Rises, The Amazing Spider-Man*), cynical dystopian futures that end with false triumph (*The Hunger Games, Prometheus*), corrupt supposed-protectors of society (*The Bourne Legacy, Safe House*), dark and twisted fairy tales (*Snow White and the Huntsman*), metaphorical worlds where the struggles of strange creatures parallel our own (*Wrath of the Titans, John Carter*), science-fiction thrillers with the hero battling government corruption (*Lockout, Total Recall*), stories that sympathize with criminals and denigrate law enforcement (*Contraband, Lawless*), and, of course, cartoons, cartoons, cartoons (*Brave, The Lorax, Madagascar 3: Europe's Most Want-*

ed, Ice Age: Continental Drift, Paranorman, Hotel Transylvania).

My theory is that the people who make movies find it difficult to remember what life was like before they integrated themselves into the Hollywood lifestyle, and, as a result, we get an awful lot of films about the kind of people with whom they are acquainted—high-rollers, wheeler-dealers, wealthy power brokers, stock-market analysts. When they want to depict people on the other end of the spectrum, they go to rebellious, misunderstood creative types—artists, writers, musicians, actors . . . and yes, filmmakers.

One I find a bit more puzzling, however, is the incredible number of movies that feature sympathetic stories or subplots about prostitutes and strippers. Really, how common is that to the average person's experience?

In 1994, a comedy called *Milk Money* went into theaters after being advertised as a picture about and, by extension, for children. The film is rated PG-13 for "sexual themes and situations involving adolescents," and in my review at the time I wrote that it portrayed "violence, sex, profanity, vulgarity, and partial nudity."

But it's the film's plot that is really outrageous: Three young suburban boys raise a hundred dollars for the sole purpose of going into the city to see a naked lady. They meet up with a prostitute who removes her blouse for them (with her back to the camera), then she drives them home with a car full of stolen cash, which brings mobsters into the mix. Back in suburbia, one of the boys plays matchmaker, trying to fix up his father with the prostitute. And in the most bizarre scene in this truly twisted movie, the boy takes the woman to his school as a visual aid for a report on the female reproductive system.

As Dave Barry likes to say when he describes something this mind-boggling, *I am not making this up.*

This was a major-studio release by Paramount Pictures with an A-list cast at the time, led by Melanie Griffith, Ed Harris, and Malcolm McDowell. But it's hard to imagine a more wrong-headed movie getting the green light and millions of dollars to be filmed and distributed. It's also hard to imagine that the people who make these kinds of decisions didn't have someone among them who questioned the wisdom of this particular project.

Movies about the common folk who make their living by selling insurance or building home fixtures or repairing automobiles or cashiering in grocery stores or working as bank tellers or librarians or secretaries or plumbers—people with whom the average moviegoer can readily identify—are quite scarce in modern movies.

And it seems a logical extension to suggest that moviemakers have forgotten what it means to retain some semblance of innocence during childhood. The result being that they throw sex, nudity, violence, and especially profanity into even the most childish film fare. Modern Hollywood moviemakers have lost touch with what it means to be a child—and especially with what the parents of "Middle America" may not want their children exposed to.

If you call them on it, filmmakers become defensive, justifying such content by arguing that children are exposed to it every day in one form or another—even in elementary schoolyards. But if you talk to teachers, or even the children themselves, they will tell you that when it is brought into the schoolyard it has often come from a movie.

Chapter 9

TRAVERSING THE HOLLYWOOD MORASS

When I was growing up in Southern California in the 1950s and '60s, my parents were avid moviegoers. We went nearly every week, to both drive-ins and "walk-ins" as we called them, and we went as a family—my mother, my father, my brother and I. There would be a cartoon, sometimes a travelogue or comedy short, an ad with dancing hot dogs encouraging us to buy snacks, and then the feature film would begin. And in those days, it was often a double feature, two movies for the price of one. It was a night out with family, a time to forget our troubles and enjoy a few hours of escapism, and we all looked forward to these little fantasy-filled getaways.

And while we had our favorite stars and types of films, we really weren't that picky about what we saw—thrillers, melodramas, musicals, westerns, comedies, science fiction, horror. As a family, our taste ran the gamut. It was all good, and often decided by who was starring. If it was James Stewart or Cary Grant or Audrey Hepburn or Doris Day or Gregory Peck or Bette Davis or James Cagney or Grace

Kelly or Robert Mitchum or anything by Alfred Hitchcock—we were there. And if it was a star that appealed more to my brother and I, my parents were fine with that, too, and we saw many movies featuring Danny Kaye, Abbott & Costello, Martin & Lewis, and Jerry Lewis solo after he broke up with Dean Martin.

As soon as I was old enough, I'd also go by myself or with friends, so I began seeing more movies than anyone else in the family. This was especially true in the 1960s when I became a teenager. My friends and I would go to movies aimed at our generation, from *Beach Party* pop-musical comedies to Edgar Allan Poe horror films to Elvis Presley rock musicals to bug-eyed-monsters-from-space pictures.

And here's the thing: My parents never worried about what I might be exposed to in any of those movies. They were designed to be entertaining and fun, and any "adult" content was subtle or oblique or hinted at or suggested; it was always a bit shaded or veiled or off-camera; it was often referred to rather than shown. There was seldom profanity beyond "hell" or "damn," and those weren't frequent. Violence didn't have gushing blood or intestines falling on the ground. Sex went on behind closed doors, and though women might wear something revealing, showing off a bit of cleavage or a bare leg, it was never graphic. And very often the films were in black and white.

Today, of course, it's a whole other ballgame. People still often pick movies because their favorite stars are in them, but they oftentimes also check out the rating. Is this one of Adam Sandler's PG-13 movies or one of his R-rated movies? Parents, but also adults for themselves, often feel they need to go through a brief education process about any movie rated PG-13 or R, because, well, it's like that song penned by Cole Porter in 1934:

In olden days, a glimpse of stocking
Was looked on as something shocking.
But now, heaven knows,
Anything goes.
Good authors too who once knew better words
Now only use four-letter words

Writing prose.
Anything goes.

"Anything goes" is right. Porter couldn't possibly have imagined what would be coming so many decades later, yet that song seems as up-to-date a commentary on modern times today as it did nearly eighty years ago. In the 21st century, it seems that parents are at war with the various forms of entertainment embraced by their children, all of which are available through venues so easy to access that it would have seemed like unbelievable science fiction when we were kids—and that's true whether you're a child of the '60s or a child of the '90s.

From newborns to seventeen-year-olds, kids today are exposed

Matthew Broderick and Mia Sara in John Hughes' Ferris Bueller's Day Off *(1986) —Paramount*

to all kinds of in-your-face violence, profanity, and sexual material on distribution modes that range from tiny handheld devices to sixty-foot IMAX screens. They're seeing and hearing things they shouldn't even be aware of until they are adults, much less be experiencing in often overwhelming visual and aural circumstances.

When my children were young in the 1970s and '80s, I tried to prevent them from seeing the really hard R-rated stuff, or for that matter, much of the hard PG, and later, PG-13 stuff, although they wanted to. The peer pressure was on. Their friends would talk up *Sixteen Candles* (1984) and *Top Gun* (1985), and even *Beverly Hills Cop* (1984) and *The Terminator* (1984), so that they felt horribly left out. Dad went to everything, so he knew what he didn't want his kids to see. *Grease* (1978)? I don't think so. *Weird Science* (1985)? No way. *National Lampoon's Vacation* (1983)? You've got to be kidding!

My kids did see a lot of movies, of course, many more than their friends, I'm sure. But they grew up on older films and still harbor a love of the Marx Brothers and Audrey Hepburn and Buster Keaton and James Stewart and Alfred Hitchcock, among many, many others. But whenever an ad for a new movie came on TV, they wanted to see that one too.

As examples, among the then-new pictures they loved were two starring Matthew Broderick, *WarGames* (1983), rated PG, and *Ferris Bueller's Day Off* (1986), rated PG-13, both featuring teenagers doing things you wouldn't want your own offspring to do. But the films were (and remain) clever, smart, funny, and exciting, and certainly more than a little enticing for children and teens (and both are still popular rental items today).

For the most part, I never worried that my kids, even the computer geniuses among them, would hack into NORAD's computers and start World War III, as in *WarGames*, and I didn't really think they'd pull a *Ferris Bueller* and feign illness to spend an entire school day impersonating an adult millionaire and driving a stolen (sort of) Ferrari.

But I was concerned about the foul language in both films, especially *Ferris Bueller*, which has profanity, obscenity, the f-word once, and a fair amount of sexual references. I was even more concerned when these films were released on VHS and the kids wanted to watch them repeatedly. They were often watching when my youngest children were around, which meant that even if a toddler wasn't really paying attention to the movie, he was still hearing all those words bounce off the walls. So, repeat viewings were quickly off the table and our home would return to its usual chaotic state, but without the questionable language. Until the next big movie came along.

The overriding question regarding films aimed at young people that have this kind of language is, why? Why are those words even in those films? Would the movies have been any less popular without the foul language? Would someone have left the theater saying, "Gee, if Ferris had cussed more that sure would have been a better movie"? Has anyone ever left a movie and complained about the lack of offensive material? Doubtful.

Oddly, there is sometimes a lot less profanity in PG movies aimed at adults, as with these: *Tootsie* (1982), *Big Business* (1988), *What About Bob*? (1991), *Groundhog Day* (1993), *Searching for Bobby Fischer* (1993), *Shadowlands* (1993), *It Could Happen to You* (1994), *Little Women* (1994), *I.Q.*, (1994), *Sense and Sensibility* (1995), *Sabrina* (1995), *Unstrung Heroes* (1995), *Emma* (1996), *The Spanish Prisoner* (1998), *Waking Ned Devine* (1998), *Return to Me* (2000), *My Big Fat Greek Wedding* (2002), *Finding Neverland* (2004), *Miss Potter* (2006), *Akeelah and the Bee* (2006), *Bright Star* (2009), *Soul Surfer* (2011), *Meek's Cutoff* (2011), *The Big Year* (2011), *We Bought a Zoo* (2011), *Won't Back Down* (2012), *Chasing Mavericks* (2012), and so on.

Wow, that's a longer list than I expected to come up with, even after I trimmed it considerably. Some of these movies do have some foul language, but considerably less than most—which illustrates that even movies aimed at adults can be successful and find their audience without resorting to unnecessary crass language. So why put such language in films aimed at youth?

I've asked many filmmakers over the years why they insert such language into their movies, and the answer is always a variation on, "Because it's realistic, that's the way people talk, especially in stressful situations." Perhaps, but a little goes a long way. And a lot becomes redundant and ineffective.

And, although Hollywood denies it, such language in movies may also contribute to the use of such language in casual conversation among young people. My grandkids tell me they hear the worst cuss words in the halls of their schools these days, especially words used over and over in movies and on TV shows.

This is another example of the incestuous nature of show business. As language on TV became more liberal in the 1970s, "damn" and "hell" and the title "God" opened a new door. Those first two words may seem extremely tame today—but the latter, with the exclamatory phrase "Oh, my God" (or, as used by texters now, "OMG") is still quite offensive to many people. And strictly on an artistic level, it's so overused that it has lost any real value in reflecting heightened tension or a character's shock or surprise.

By the 1980s, excessively coarse language on television programs had begun to take hold as writers and producers were looking for whatever words they felt they could get away with. Meanwhile, their competitors were looking to copy whatever the other guy did get away with.

I first noticed this when the word "ass" began to creep into commercial TV shows. It somehow became acceptable on the air as an expletive and also as a descriptive term to disparage someone—and before long it was being used on every other show. Even kids shows. In fact, that word became so noticeable and commonplace that I began to laugh whenever it was used, not because it was funny, but because it was so ridiculous. It was completely gratuitous and out of place, as if the characters were simply saying it like a defiant child: "Since you don't want me to say it, I'm going to say it all the time!" David Letterman still too often uses this particular word as a punchline, as if it is inherently funny. It's not.

Around the same time, "sucks" entered the TV vernacular, despite how off-putting it was when it started. Along with the words "bitch" and "wussy," later reduced to "wuss." But these days these exclamations and many others that are even more offensive are so commonplace that no one even seems to notice anymore, much less flinch. Slowly, many more objectionable words have entered the commercial-TV lexicon in the same way. And perhaps, the first time you heard one of them you thought to yourself, "Oh, well, there's another new one, and now everyone on TV will start saying it." And you were right.

Are TV writers really so desperate that they watch other shows to steal whatever pseudo-profanities have been let in the door? I think that's exactly what happens. And moviemakers apparently do the same thing. How else does one explain a word that is heard on one program or in one movie, which then suddenly becomes so overused in every other show and film, that you're hearing it all the time.

To illustrate, let's set aside the obvious profanities and obscenities and vulgarities that have been common in movie vernacular for longer than I can remember, and take as an example of things that kids pick up from TV and movies the phrase "douchebag," (sometimes reduced to "douche"). This is now commonly used as an epithet, an insulting term that refers to someone, usually male, who is deliberately and arrogantly inconsiderate or unkind, along the lines of calling someone a "stupid jerk."

The word has been occasionally used as an insult in literature dating back at least to the 1950s, and the first time I noticed it in a movie was in *E.T.: The Extra-Terrestrial* in 1982, when a young boy says "douchbag" as an insult. In that scene, the boy's utterance prompts an adult to chide him, saying she won't have that kind of language in her home (a consequence of the kind that is sadly lacking in most modern movies). At the time, the word's use seemed to be an anomaly. But, it has for some reason, really taken hold as a pejorative term in the 2000s, and now it's everywhere, used constantly in the entertainment media—to such a degree that its usage has become ridiculous.

But what drove it home was one day when I was visiting my oldest daughter and her family, and I was rather startled to hear my teenage grandson refer to someone as a "douchebag." So I asked him if he knew what it meant, and he said, no, not really. I suggested he look up the definition before using it again, and he went straight to the computer and an online dictionary, then returned quite embarrassed after finding the clinical definition of a device used for vaginal cleansing.

Continuing the conversation, and trying to allay my grandson's embarrassment, I asked where he had heard the word. He said he first heard it on a couple of TV shows, though he couldn't recall which, and that it wasn't long before everyone at school was saying it. OK, this is anecdotal, not in the least bit scientific. But it would seem that, at least in this case, the word gained acceptance based on its use in the media.

Filmmakers have told me repeatedly over the years that there's no proof that kids pick things up from movies or TV. And that's actually true. There is no proof. There are many research studies that are touted as evidence on one side and debunked as flawed on the other. You can find studies that say kids do pick things up from movies and you can find just as many that say such results are inconclusive. Whether sex or foul language in movies can motivate young people to emulate what they see and hear is still up for debate.

Violence, on the other hand, is becoming perhaps less of a question. For decades now, the connection between violence and various forms of media has been more heavily researched and there has been evidence shown that, for example, movie, TV, and videogame violence may prompt young children to become more aggressive.

On an adult level, the possible link between movies and violence may also be more accepted today simply because there are some indisputable examples of violent acts being related to specific films—from the 1974 Hi-Fi Shop murders in Ogden, Utah, to the 2012 movie-theater shootings in Aurora, Colorado. In the former, victims were forced to drink Drano, which the killers said they were inspired to use because it worked effectively in a scene from the Dirty Harry movie *Magnum Force*, which they had watched repeatedly while plotting the robbery. The Aurora killings occurred in a movie-theater auditorium during a midnight screening of *The Dark Knight Rises* and reportedly the gunman had dyed his hair red and was calling himself the Joker, which was the villain in the previous Batman movie, *The Dark Knight*.

After the Aurora incident, many people in the film industry were surprised when Harvey Weinstein (the same film executive that protested the R-ratings for *The King's Speech* and *Bully*) seemed to acknowledge that violent movies may indeed influence people like the Colorado shooter.

Weinstein—under whose aegis such ultra-violent films as *True Romance*, *Pulp Fiction*, and *Django Unchained*, among many others, have been released—called for the industry to rethink the often brutal violence of modern movies. Weinstein told the Huffington Post in July 2012 that filmmakers "can't shirk our responsibility" for depicting violence in popular movies, and he spoke out in favor of gun control. Weinstein also suggested a summit on the subject: "We should sit down—the Marty Scorseses, the Quentin Tarantinos, and hopefully all of us who deal in violence in movies—and discuss our role in that." Whether anything will come of Weinstein's suggestions remains to be seen.

This subject of whether violent acts seen in the media influence young people has been a long-running debate going back to the gangster movies of the 1930s, but it took on new impetus in the 1950s as children were more frequently exposed to such films on television, as well as comic violence in everything from the Three Stooges shorts to Daffy Duck cartoons. And then again in the 1980s, as movies became more realistic in their portrayal of violence, and depictions of splattering blood and guts were being shown in greater numbers than ever before.

Over the years quite a few studies have gathered data about how many killings the average child would see in movies, TV shows, cartoons, and comic books/graphic novels—and later, video games and online videos—numbers reaching into the multiple thousands. But whether the effect on young minds is damaging has always been a point of contention. For every Senate subcommittee hearing on juvenile delinquency that has decried mass media's obsession with violence and made its findings public to shock and outrage, there has been someone more than willing to question the methodology and try to debunk the results.

As far as I can tell, nothing in the movies has changed in all that time, except that violence has become more graphic than ever in many adult films. And in PG-13 movies, while it may be less graphic and bloody, violence has certainly grown in terms of body count and jokey killings, as attested to by everything from James Bond and Arnold Schwarzenegger to *Hanna* and *The Dark Knight Rises.*

As mentioned, there has not been nearly as much research on sex and language in movies and whether it affects young people, and what studies there are never seem to take hold for very long, especially in

Clark Gable and Claudette Colbert in Frank Capra's It Happened One Night *(1934) —Columbia*

the Hollywood community. It's hard to get the public on your side when something is "proven" by one study only to be contradicted by the next. Eggs are good for you, eggs are bad for you. Whatever.

My response to this has always been that if filmmakers and TV executives really believe no one can be influenced by what they see in a movie or on television, then what's the point of advertising? After all, if they believe a thirty-second commercial can persuade consumers to attend a certain movie or buy a particular truck or purchase a different brand of toothpaste or switch their car insurance, how can they believe a two-hour movie or a half-hour sitcom has no influence at all?

And what about clothing styles that change because of movies? Hats, glasses, mini-skirts, midi-skirts, whether men should wear T-shirts or women should wear bras—these kinds of fashion statements have influenced everyday Americans since movies began.

When Katharine Hepburn wore trousers in *Bringing Up Baby* (1938), pants sales for women rose tremendously. Audrey Hepburn's sleek, sleeveless eveningwear became fashionable in the 1950s. Diane Keaton's mix-and-match chic became popular after *Annie Hall* (1977). The braless look was popularized in the 1920s and early '30s, then faded for a few decades, only to return in the 1970s for a brief time. And on the men's side, in 1934 when Clark Gable revealed in the Oscar-winning *It Happened One Night* that he was not wearing a T-shirt under his dress shirt, undershirt sales famously plummeted. Then, in 1955, white T-shirts were back in style after James Dean wore one under his jacket in *Rebel Without a Cause.* And modern teenagers copy the clothing and hairstyles of their favorite stars just as often today as they did when Elvis was king.

There has also been research about movies romanticizing smoking, suggesting that when they see their favorite movie stars casually puffing on cigarettes and cigars onscreen, young people who might not otherwise think about smoking tend to light up. The anti-smoking lobby exerted such tremendous pressure on CARA that the board eventually changed its thinking so that smoking is now the newest element of content evaluated for movie ratings. Which would seem to be validation from inside the industry for arguments about whether movies have an effect on young people.

Despite claims to the contrary by filmmakers, it's obvious that kids often pick things up from movies and TV, to include slang and attitude, and perhaps negative social habits, which causes me to worry about all the sexually charged material they are exposed to repeatedly in every form of media. It's hard to believe that watching movies over and over again that depict recreational sex as perfectly acceptable, especially those that show teenagers having sex, doesn't exert some influence over young viewers.

It's easy to generalize in chiding the entire entertainment industry, but we must acknowledge that there are some artists who seem to be aware of what the industry is doing, and who even comment on it in their own small way, as if to say, "Hey, we're not all blind or insensitive to the crassness in the media."

I confess to being quite taken aback at a moment in Sandra Bullock's Oscar-winning PG-13 film *The Blind Side* (2009), as her character's husband uses the word "ass"—and she calls him on it. A friend suggested that perhaps the scene is meant as sarcasm, to mock those of us who care about such things, a subtle way of calling us prudes. I didn't see it that way and, even if it's true, I don't care. I was glad to see it, and I prefer to interpret it as a comment on how language in casual conversation is becoming more and more coarse, and that we need to be reminded to take the high road.

Another 2009 picture, the animated film *The Fantastic Mr. Fox* offers an alternative to swearing. There's a terrific running gag that has the characters, instead of using profane words, saying "cuss." That is, they actually use the word "cuss" as a substitute for cussing. "What the cuss?" Mr. Fox says. And every other character moved to proclaim a profanity also says "cuss" instead. And not just the anthropomorphic animals but the humans, too. It's hilarious, and points out just how silly it is to use the same words over and over as exclamations.

Thinking about it, when I was a kid it was common to refer to someone as a cuss. "That ornery old cuss," my dad would say about a grouchy neighbor. No question. "Cuss" would be a much more pleasant substitute than some of the words we actually hear in movies.

Then there were the pithy and memorable comments made in the early 1980s by Richard D. Heffner when he was still the head of CARA. In Stephen Vaughn's book *Freedom and Entertainment: Rating the Movies in an Age of New Media*, the author writes:

> Appalled by what he and other rating board members were seeing each week, dismayed that the self-restraint needed from moviemakers to make voluntarism work seemed in short supply, he acknowledged his 'own sense of shame for humanity that other human beings actually create and distribute and exhibit media content that so taints everything and perhaps everyone it touches.' To a London audience in 1982, and again in Toronto two years later, he said, 'I do dearly wish the earth would just open up to swallow whole some of the dreadful things we see . . . perhaps even some of the dreadful persons who make them.'

From its first feature-length movie released in 1937, the Walt Disney Company label on a film has meant one thing: This is family-friendly. Even as other studios were growing up, as it were, and starting to release films with questionable content, Disney remained in the family trenches. If it said "Disney," the entire family could attend without worry—and that was true all the way through most of the 1970s.

In January 1979, however, came the first experiment with more mature-themed movies at the Mouse House. The independent comedy-drama *Take Down*, starring Edward Herrmann as a high school English teacher reluctantly recruited to coach the wrestling team, went to theaters nationally via Disney's distribution arm Buena Vista.

This was the first PG-rated movie handled by the company, although the Disney brand did not appear on the film.

The first official PG-rated Disney movie with that label prominently attached was a *Star Wars*-inspired space saga titled *The Black Hole*, released in December 1979. Its second PG-rated movie was *Midnight Madness* in 1980, but that one went out without the Disney name, a la *Take Down*.

Over the next few years, several PG-rated Disney films followed, including *The Watcher in the Woods* (1980), *Condorman* (1981), *The Devil and Max Devlin* (1981), *Dragonslayer* (1981), *Tron* (1982), *Night Crossing* (1982), *Tex* (1982), *Never Cry Wolf* (1983), *Something Wicked This Way Comes* (1983), *Trenchcoat* (1983), *The Journey of Natty Gann* (1985), *Return to Oz* (1985), *Flight of the Navigator* (1986), and *The Black Cauldron* (1986)—the latter was also distinguished as the studio's first PG-rated animated feature.

But to go any further in the 1980s was up for debate as Disney was still nervous about sullying the brand, so an "adult" production company was created, Touchstone, for more adult-oriented films. The first release for Disney's new movie subsidiary was the mermaid comedy *Splash* (1984), starring Tom Hanks and Daryl Hannah. The PG-rated movies listed above might use the words "hell" or "damn," they might have a bit more violence or dark themes and maybe just a tad of salacious innuendo, but they are squeaky-clean compared to the PG-rated *Splash*, which contains nudity, profanity, vulgarity, and sexual innuendo, as well as some violence. And *Splash* did indeed make a big splash—it was a significant box-office hit, ushering in a new era for Disney, one that was here to stay.

Touchstone films that immediately followed were fairly benign, the PG-rated *Country* (1984), *Baby: Secret of the Lost Legend* (1985), and *My Science Project* (1985). But then came a turning point for the company. In January 1986 came the raunchy, foul-mouthed *Down and Out in Beverly Hills* (1986), the first R-rated movie produced by Disney . . . er, Touchstone. And it was another box-office hit, ensuring that many more would follow. In fact, these films proved so successful that one "adult" movie arm was not enough, so Disney formed yet another, Hollywood Pictures, which was initiated with the PG-13 rated *Arachnophobia* (1990), and would also include R-rated films on its roster.

But the studio kept the "Disney" name for more family-friendly fare, although in the 1990s the definition of "family-friendly" was expanded to include films with questionable content for children and teens. The first signal that Disney's chaste walls were crumbling arrived in 1990 with the spoofy, stylish Warren Beatty comic-strip adaptation *Dick Tracy*, co-starring Madonna. That film was slated to be a Walt Disney Pictures release, but at the last minute the studio became skittish about the film's level of violence and sexual innuendo, so it became a Touchstone picture, even after it was rated PG instead of PG-13.

The following year, however, such fears were set aside when, against all odds, *The Rocketeer* also received a PG, despite an equally large, if bloodless, body count, some verbal innuendo, and a camera that seems to enjoy focusing on Jennifer Connelly's cleavage. It was released as a Walt Disney Picture and the gloves were off.

Touchstone and Hollywood Pictures are still in place for many Disney studio releases, but these days, for good or ill, the "Disney" name occasionally hovers over PG-13 movies as violent as *John Carter* (2012) and the *Pirates of the Caribbean* franchise (four films from 2003 to 2011, with No. 5 on the way), but for the most part it maintains the standard it had in the olden days when I was growing up, which is to say, when you see "Disney" above a title it still means that that movie is likely to be more family-friendly and certainly cleaner than anything else out there, as exemplified by the majority of Disney-labeled product: *The Odd Life of Timothy Green* (2012), *The Muppets* (2011), *Secretariat* (2010), *Enchanted* (2007), *Miracle* (2004) and myriad others.

Cynics may roll their eyes, but for my part I'm happy to see someone still producing—if I may use an old-fashioned phrase—some good, clean, wholesome entertainment.

Not that we shouldn't be wary anyway and check out Disney releases as we would any other movies. And that also goes for other studios that label their pictures as family films.

Take for example a straight-to-video title I received for review in 2006, *Bring It On: All or Nothing*, the third in the *Bring It On* competitive-cheerleading movie series (five so far). The first on-screen credit for *All or Nothing* reads: "Universal Studios Family Productions." That it is rated PG-13 provides a red flag, of course, but the "Family Productions" credit led me to believe . . . fleetingly . . . that this might indeed be a family-friendly picture.

In a pre-credits sequence is the obligatory flatulence joke—hardly unexpected in comedies aimed at young people these days—but then, within the first 10 minutes, the heroine is assuring her boyfriend that she'll give up her virginity to him on prom night. Yikes! Is this really what Hollywood considers "family" fare these days?

To be fair, this *Bring It On* sequel isn't nearly as raunchy as it could be, and there is a nice message about racial tolerance. But that just makes the sexual material all the more ill thought out.

When a movie is labeled as "family entertainment" or targets youngsters in its ad campaigns, parents should be able to feel safe allowing their kids to see it. But an ever-growing mountain of evidence proves you can't simply take Hollywood's word for it.

Many movies have received PG or PG-13 ratings, despite having adult themes that are obviously not intended for children or teenagers—not necessarily because of content, but simply because they are adult-oriented in terms of theme or subject. Not that young people can't get something out of them, but these films are clearly not aimed at them. And as I've brought some of them into this book's discussion, I have not meant to suggest they should all be rated R.

Quite often we still get a *Driving Miss Daisy* (1989) or an *Apollo 13* (1995), or *The First Wives Club* (1996), all rated PG—and there are many more, all of them perfectly fine as they stand. But they do sometimes serve to lull the moviegoing audience into thinking they can see other films with these ratings and not be shocked or appalled, which, of course, is simply not the case.

As mentioned earlier, in the 1980s I was asking whether *The Blues Brothers* or *Ordinary People*, each rated R for a few cuss words, should have the same rating as the extremely violent *Friday the 13th* or the extremely sexual and profane *Used Cars*? Today, we might ask if the PG-13 ratings applied to *The Blind Side* (2009) for some language and violence, or in *The Artist* (2012), for an aborted suicide attempt, should be the same as the extremely sexual and crude *Crazy, Stupid, Love* (2011) or the extremely dark and violent *The Dark Knight Rises* (2012)?

The shift in mores between 1980 and 2012 is obvious, but the movie industry seems to have painted itself into a corner with the rating system as it stands today. Despite protestations to the contrary by CARA and the MPAA, it really is all about box office revenue. If these movies had received R ratings, they might not have been nearly as successful. True, extremely hard R-rated movies like *Bridesmaids* (2011), the two *Hangover* films (2009/2011) and *Ted* (2012), among others, were big hits, but they are the exception, not the rule.

In general, the R rating tends to chase a portion of the audience away. And that's the real reason more PG-13 movies don't receive R ratings for what is clearly adult material. The bottom line is all about the bottom line. Money, that is to say, profits, drive moviemaking just like any other business. It may be an art form, but it's mostly a business. And if you look at the top one hundred box-office moneymakers of any year, you'll see that G, PG, and PG-13 movies dominate by roughly seventy-five percent, while R-rated films make up about a quarter, and few of those are in the top fifty, much less the top ten.

In 2011, the top one hundred hits included twenty-four R-rated movies. Only eight of those were in the top fifty and only one was in the top ten. And that's pretty much the average every year.

So, the next time you see a news report that says, as if for the first time, that a new study reveals R-rated movies, as a rule, do not perform as well as movies with ratings that allow entrance by audience members under eighteen—and you will see such a story, since they come around every year—it won't be news to you.

It's also worth noting that in addition to rising prices for movie tickets, box-office lists today are a bit skewed because some movies make additional money from surcharges added to showings in 3D and on IMAX screens or with DBox seats (which shake like amusement-park rides during action films). As a result, if you look at "adjusted" box-office charts, those that measure numbers of tickets sold—which better indicate how many people attended a given film—as opposed to the dollar amounts earned by each film, it offers a very different picture.

On the all-time moneymakers chart, *Avatar* is in the number one spot. But on the adjusted-for-inflation chart, which better indicates how many people saw the film in a theater, *Avatar* drops to fourteen. The film attended by the most people in movie history is, and has been forever, *Gone With the Wind* (1939), while *Star Wars* (1977) is number two. Those that follow in the top ten are *The Sound of Music* (1965), *E.T.: The Extra-Terrestrial* (1982), *Titanic* (1997, to include the 2012 3D reissue), *The Ten Commandments* (1956), *Jaws* (1975), *Doctor Zhivago* (1965), *The Exorcist* (1973), and *Snow White and the Seven Dwarfs* (1937).

As you can see, the R-rated horror film *The Exorcist* is at number nine on the adjusted list, but it is one of only ten R-rated movies in the top one hundred, and one of only four in the top fifty.

From all this it becomes evident that movies with graphic adult material are the least attended of all movies made. And yet each year, R-rated movies comprise at least a third of all theatrical releases. It doesn't make business sense, but it speaks to the studios' conflict with the "artists" who make the movies, and whose liberal sensibilities inform the way they make them.

Another curious Hollywood moneymaking ploy is the editing of movies for venues outside movie theaters.

Everyone knows about the harder versions of movies that are frequently released on home video, a PG-13 movie that has been taken to the R-rated level, or an R-rated movie that becomes "unrated" because footage was added to make the movie more harsh than the version rated by CARA. They often show up on DVD and Blu-ray as "special editions" or "director's cuts."

But movies are also edited into softer versions to make them more acceptable to wider audiences, which, of course, means so that kids can watch them. They show up from time to time on TV channels that won't screen gory violence or graphic sex or nudity or most foul language (yes, there are still a few channels like that), and they are also seen on airline flights. Movies shown on planes have been edited by the studios to delete offensive material, but then these toned-down versions return to the studio vaults and are never seen again. In other words, the more harsh versions of movies frequently find their way to home video, but softer versions never do.

Fred Crane, Vivien Leigh and George Reeves in Victor Fleming's Gone with the Wind *(1939) —MGM*

Over the years, I've heard many stories from people who watched an "airline cut" movie on a flight, loved it and later looked to rent it for family viewing, only to be shocked by R-rated content that wasn't in the version seen on the plane. An example of my own was *Music Within* (2007), a little true drama about hearing-impaired Richard Pimentel, a real-life advocate for the disabled, a film laced with wit and humor, and which I found tremendously moving and heartfelt.

Watching it on a very small screen on the back of the seat in front of me during an international flight in 2008, I didn't notice any editing blips, and I didn't think twice about ordering the DVD when I got home so I could share it with family and friends. But when it arrived, I noticed the R rating, and watching it again I was disappointed by the amount of profanity it contained. Many an f-bomb was dropped. So much for sharing it with others.

Since *Music Within* never played in theaters outside Los Angeles and New York, and, therefore, failed to make a dent at the box office, would it have been that difficult to include the edited version on the DVD alongside the R-rated version? Given that choice, I would have enthusiastically recommended it. But "airline cuts" just go away after they run their course on the air-travel circuit.

When I've asked filmmakers or studio chiefs why these softened versions of movies don't go to home video, they always say that the director, the "artist" who made the movie, doesn't want any other version to be released, preferring that the "official" theatrical release be the only one out there. If that's true, why are these edited versions shown at all? Why are the films softened for limited runs on TV, on airline flights, in hotel rooms, and other such venues? Why aren't the filmmakers protesting those usages? And if they're so obsessed with the "original" theatrical version, why are their movies edited to be rougher for home video?

There's really no sound reason for keeping airline cuts out of circulation, especially if it is looked at in a business sense. It's not like the studios would have to go to great expense to release them. These edited versions already exist. Beyond transferring them to DVDs there's really no extra cost to speak of. And with today's technology they could easily be included with the "official" versions on the same disc. Seems to me like a missed revenue opportunity.

Movie ratings are not completely without value. One can generally assume that a teen comedy rated R is going to contain more offensive material than a teen comedy rated PG. And a teen comedy rated PG-13 is going to be somewhere in between and might take a bit of research to determine whether your child should see it.

Years at this job have taught me that some parents don't care about nudity or sex in films, but don't want their children exposed to excessive violence, while other parents will let their kids see very violent films, but don't want them exposed to sex or nudity. Others still are more bothered by language than anything else, but some don't care how much foul language is in a movie as long as it's clean in other ways. And some people, of course, don't care about any of this. But for those of us who do, it's important to pay attention, especially when the kids are going on and on about something they want to see.

Movie ratings are for parents, or so we're told, but the truth is a lot of parents have given up on the rating system. Many don't even look at the ratings before deciding what to go see, or what to let their children see. And this was never more evident than when, in the summer of 2012, a comedy opened in theaters with the simple title *Ted*—a very R-rated movie from Seth MacFarlane, creator and voice star of the raunchy TV cartoon sitcom *The Family Guy*.

Ted, MacFarlane's first film (and a big box-office hit) is a live-action comedy about yet another adult male stuck in adolescence (Mark Wahlberg), who, as a child, made a Christmas wish that brought his beloved teddy bear to life. Twenty-seven years later the teddy bear is still his best friend and roommate, and it is also a foul-mouthed, pot-smoking womanizer.

According to news accounts shortly after the film's release, a number of parents around the country took their children to see *Ted*, which they perceived as simply a family movie about a cute talking teddy bear, in some cases after being nagged by their children who had glimpsed a clip from the film on TV. But after a few minutes in the theater, these parents picked up the kids and bolted for the exit.

The film does carry an R rating, which is clearly printed on the posters, albeit small, in a corner. There were two different posters available for display in movie theaters. One does appear to be inviting to families, as it shows Wahlberg sitting with the teddy bear on a couch, both facing the camera and laughing together, as if watching TV. This was the poster that could be used by theaters that didn't want to show the other poster, which depicts Wahlberg and the bear with their backs to us as they stand at urinals in a public restroom. (And oddly similar to the poster for Adam Sandler's 1999 comedy *Big Daddy*, which shows Sandler and a young child with their backs to the camera, apparently urinating in an outdoor setting.)

The *Ted* trailers, however, leave no room for doubt that this is an adults-only film. There's Ted the teddy bear smoking a bong, there's Ted posing for a photo with three girls in a park and his hand is on one girl's breast, there's Ted using the word "bastard" as an expletive, there's Ted simulating a sexual act with a credit-card machine on a checkstand counter . . . and that's just in the green-band trailer, a preview that might be shown before any movie you go to see. The red-band trailer, shown only with R-rated movies, is even more specific, with multiple f-bombs, and extended, more specific versions of the scenes described above.

Anecdotally, I wonder if very many theaters around the country actually played a trailer for *Ted*. I go to the movies every week, sometimes more than once a week, and I never saw a trailer for *Ted* precede any movie I attended in the months leading up to its release. To write about it here, I relied on Google to find it for me.

In 1984, David Sterritt, (movie critic for the *Christian Science Monitor* until his retirement in 2005) wrote that the then-brand-new PG-13 was a step in the right direction, adding, "But the real answer to protection problems is for parents to take the PG initials at their face value—to read reviews, check with friends and neighbors, phone theaters with specific questions, and generally provide the 'parental guidance' that's needed. If parents shouldered more of the guidance burden themselves, they could expect less from—and be better served by—the shorthand of the rating system."

Fast-forward to 2012 and Roger Ebert (who still reviews movies for the *Chicago Sun-Times*) wrote at the end of his review for *Ted*: "I must end on a note of warning. *Ted* is not merely an R-rated movie, but a very R-rated movie—'for crude and sexual content, pervasive language and some drug use,' according to the MPAA, and what they mean by 'some' is hard to figure, because it could hardly contain more. No matter how much kids want to see the teddy bear movie in the ads on TV, steer them to *Brave*. Trust me on this."

These are just two examples of efforts by members of the media to inform their readers about what's going on with movies. But whom do you trust?

There are lots of online sites that discuss movies and claim to be family-friendly, and some are better at it than others. If you are looking for the specifics, counting cuss words, describing sex scenes, explaining the level of violence, there are lots of those. If you want a more measured view, those are out there, too. If you just want to know if critics are finding a particular film good, bad, or ugly, there are even more of those.

Each of the sites listed below has many more applications than are listed here, but for our purposes these descriptions refer strictly to movie-content evaluation:

★ www.imdb.com—The Internet Movie Database has individual pages for each movie title, and each page includes a "Parents Guide" link that says "View Content Advisory." For many titles, especially older films, the page is blank. But for the latest releases and a growing number of older films, the information is often quite specific.

- ★ www.movieguide.org—Movie Guide offers specific information from a Christian perspective and rates language, violence, sex, and nudity on a four-bullet scale from "none" to "heavy."

- ★ www.pluggedin.com—Plugged In is another Christian-oriented site, reviewing movies with breakout sections on "positive elements" and "spiritual content," as well as sexual, violent, crude or profane language, drug and alcohol, and other negative content.

- ★ www.kids-in-mind.com—Kids in Mind rates movies according to content, with a rating bar for "sex & nudity," "violence & gore," and "profanity," as well as specific descriptions of content as related to these and other areas of evaluation.

- ★ www.parentpreviews.com—Parent Previews evaluates various kinds of movie content on an A, B, C, D grade scale, an A indicating no violence or sex or whatever category is being graded, while a D means there is a lot. Each area is fleshed out with descriptions, though they seem in general to be a bit less explicit than some sites.

- ★ www.commonsensemedia.org—Common Sense Media includes a descriptive paragraph for movie content, as well as a chart that gives from one to five bullets for each of these categories: "Positive messages," "Positive role models," "Violence," "Sex," "Language," "Consumerism," and "Drinking, drugs & smoking."

- ★ www.parentalguide.org—Parental Guide offers overviews/reviews of films rated G, PG, and PG-13, and discusses content along the way, less explicitly than some sites, and R-rated movies are not evaluated.

★ www.screenit.com—Screen It reviews some 150 new movies yearly, each with a content summary and 15 categories of specific descriptive content. I must confess that I have not actually used this site because—whereas those listed above are free—this one requires membership, asks for credit-card information, and charges a $7.95 monthly fee or $47 for a year in advance.

For people looking for reliable movie reviews, I would suggest checking out www.rottentomatoes.com and www.metacritic.com—two aggregate sites that collect movie reviews from around the country and give each film an overall collective rating based on the number of positive vs. negative reviews. Each site also links to many full-length reviews ranging from the *New York Times* and the *Los Angeles Times* to less well known online critics. Reading some reviews will tell you if you're on the same wavelength with certain critics and that might help you use them to make informed judgment calls about whether a new film is something you or your children want to see.

TV shows and video games have their own rating systems:

Explanations of content ratings that show up on the screen at the beginning of television programs can be found at Reboot, an FCC site; this is the page that explains the TV rating system: http://transition.fcc.gov/vchip/#guidelines

Explanations of content ratings on packaging for video games can be found at the Entertainment Software Rating Board (ESRB) site: http://www.esrb.org/ratings/ratings_guide.jsp

Chapter 10

HOLLYWOOD STILL MAKES GOOD MOVIES

In Spite of Itself

Emails frequently come my way asking for movie recommendations, and when I'm with friends—or strangers, for that matter—I am often asked for titles they can safely watch with other family members without being embarrassed. I'm also quizzed, and sometimes challenged, about what I think of particular movies. All of which is fine. It comes with the territory. Most are just trying to find something fairly new from the past few years, something they haven't seen, and something that's both good and clean. All of which really narrows the field.

Although I wrote my first professional critique at the *Deseret News* in 1978, my movie-reviewing days actually go back to when I was a young teenager. Because I saw so many movies, often several each week, I found myself being approached by adults—my parents' friends, the neighbors—asking what I thought of particular movies that were playing locally, and I was more than happy to share my teenage opinions. Back in those days, however, and even later as a young adult, I never thought about commenting on a film's potentially offensive content. I just said what I thought of the movie, citing something good, bad, or indifferent and left it at that.

By the time I began reviewing movies professionally, however, questions about my opinion were often followed by a query regarding content—Why is it rated R? How much profanity does it have? Is the sex graphic? How bloody is the violence?—that kind of thing. So I began thinking about movies in broader terms. After all, my job at the *Deseret News* was to serve readers, to supply information to help them decide what to spend their hard-earned entertainment dollars on. And I took it seriously.

But as the years passed it became more and more difficult to find movies I could casually recommend. Once, when I was asked by a prominent church leader what film I'd suggest for him to see with his wife, meaning something in theaters at that moment, I responded flippantly, joking that they'd be safer watching an old movie at home. He wasn't going to let me off the hook that easily, though, and said he was serious. He and his wife wanted to go to the movies, but were leery about just randomly choosing something out of the array at the multiplex. So I thought for a moment and came up with a couple of choices I felt were safe. And then I followed up later with a list of newer films on home video they also might enjoy.

As the years passed, I began receiving so many email requests for recent titles on DVD that were clean enough to watch with the family, that I began keeping track as such films rolled around. And a couple of years ago I compiled a lengthy list for a column—movies from the past 20 years rated PG. That prompted readers to start sending me their suggestions, and so another column or two followed. And that was the genesis of this chapter.

Although parents worry about all the garbage that seems to flow in and out of movie complexes these days, and feel a bit flummoxed by the long lists of titles they see on Netflix or other rental sites, let me assure you that there really are good, clean movies released every year. Sometimes, they don't stick around in theaters for very long, and it's often hard to find them in the morass of titles listed in a massive online directory—what the heck was that movie called?—but they're out there. It just requires a little more effort to find them rather than simply settling for whatever is available at the top of your online queue or whichever title is being pushed by the vendor this week or the latest box-office smash or whatever happens to be "hot" right now . . . zombies, vampires, superheroes . . .

Don't let Hollywood decide what you watch. You decide. And to help, this chapter is comprised of similar overlong, bedeviling lists of movie titles—all from the past two decades and nearly all rated G or PG (a few PG-13s have slipped in). These are movies that I feel comfortable recommending, some for family viewing, some for adults, and in terms of content, most have a bit of cursing and others may have some mild violence, but compared to the bulk of modern mov-

Asa Butterfield and Chloë Grace Mortez in Martin Scorsese's Hugo *(2011) — Paramount*

ies, they are very clean. And it is hoped that you'll be able to find something—perhaps a lot of somethings—to enjoy from these suggestions.

I've stayed away from the blockbusters. I don't have to tell you about *Home Alone* or *Harry Potter* or *National Treasure* or *How to Train Your Dragon* or *Diary of a Wimpy Kid* or the latest from Pixar—you know about those. And you may ask, "What about such favorites as *The Hunt for Red October* or *Enchanted*?" since they are also rated PG, but, again, those are such widely known, still popular, well-remembered, and often-rented titles that I haven't felt the need to include them here.

These movies are meant to make you aware of something you may have missed or remind you of something you may have enjoyed but forgotten. And the mini-reviews are my personal opinions, so take them or leave them. But, hopefully, you'll find enough to lead you to some excellent adventures. In fact, in the effort of compiling these lists, I've reminded myself of quite a few that we'll be watching soon at my house.

The rating explanations are also my own interpretations. And everything here is available on DVD or Blu-ray or such online streaming sites as Netflix or Crackle or On Demand or iTunes or Amazon.com or Hulu or myriad others, some free and some requiring a rental fee.

These movies start in 2012 and go back through the 1990s, with titles grouped as movies that families can enjoy together and those that are more adult, but of course you may decide to watch some of those with your kids, too. In the 2000s there is also a separate list of sports films, simply because during that decade there was an unusual number of clean family movies revolving around competitive games.

MOVIES FROM THE 2000s

FOR FAMILIES:

★ *The Odd Life of Timothy Green* (2012, PG, should be rated G): A couple (Jennifer Garner, Joel Edgerton) wishes for a child of their own and the title character (CJ Adams) sprouts up, literally, from their garden. Funny supporting performance from Dianne Wiest.

★ *Big Miracle* (2012, PG, some profanity): Touching, sometimes amusing true story of whales stuck in Arctic ice, with all-star cast (led by John Krasinski and Drew Barrymore) attempting a rescue.

★ *We Bought a Zoo* (2011, PG, profanity): Matt Damon stars in this based-on-a-true-story comedy-drama of a widower with two children who impulsively buys a dilapidated zoo and then struggles to get it ready for public inspection with the help of longtime employees.

★ *Hugo* (2011, PG, mild violence): The cleanest movie ever made by Martin Scorsese is set in 1930s Paris and follows a young orphaned boy who operates the clock tower. Eventually his life intersects with a shopkeeper revealed to be George Méliès, a real-life innovative filmmaker at the dawn of cinema. Fanciful, colorful, and often quite humorous.

★ *Dolphin Tale* (2011, PG, should be rated G): Loosely based on the true story of a bottlenose dolphin that lost its tail in a crab trap and how it comes to be fitted with a prosthetic. Bolstered by the presence of Ashley Judd, Harry Connick Jr., and especially Morgan Freeman.

★ *Hachi: A Dog's Tale* (2010, G): Excellent, based on a true story. Richard Gere adopts a dog that waits for him at the train station every day for the rest of his life—and beyond.

- ★ *Eight Below* (2006, PG, animal violence, mild language): Sled-dog trainer Paul Walker can't leave his eight dogs behind when a U.S. research team is ordered to leave its Antarctic base, so he resolves to save them.

- ★ *Ella Enchanted* (2004, PG, mild violence, mild vulgarity): Anne Hathaway is a "Cinderella" character, the victim of a spell that requires her to do whatever she is told in this cute fairy tale spoof.

- ★ *Secondhand Lions* (2003, PG, foul language, violence): Wonderful, touching story of a young boy (Haley Joel Osment) left with his two reclusive uncles (Robert Duvall, Michael Caine) who regale him with stories of their youthful adventures.

- ★ *The School of Rock* (2003, PG-13, mild language): Arguably, Jack Black's best movie has him pretending to be a substitute teacher to recruit nerdy fifth-grade musicians to fulfill his own delusional rock-band dreams. Hilarious, especially Joan Cusack as the suspicious principal.

- ★ *My Dog Skip* (2000, PG, mild violence, language): True story of a young boy (Frankie Muniz) growing up in 1940s Mississippi who has trouble coming out of his shell until he receives a pet dog that helps him connect with others. Funny and touching, with Diane Lane and Kevin Bacon as the boy's parents.

FOR PARENTS:

- ★ *War Horse* (2011, PG-13, wartime violence, a few mild profanities): Steven Spielberg's compelling tale of a thoroughbred trained by a farmboy, their separation during

World War I, and the surprising circumstances that ultimately bring them back together.

★ *The Big Year* (2011, PG, profanity): Steve Martin, Jack Black, and Owen Wilson are competing birders (don't call them birdwatchers) in this sweet, gentle comedy with something to say about personal growth and pursuing your passion. With a wonderful cast of older actors in support: Dianne Wiest, Brian Dennehy, JoBeth Williams, Anjelica Huston, Kevin Pollak, and (the voice of) John Cleese.

★ *Meek's Cutoff* (2011, PG, mild violence, mild language): Very low-key pioneer tale is a slow but richly measured character study of three families crossing the Oregon Trail in 1845, and the mountain man whose shortcut proves disastrous. Quite rewarding for the patient viewer. Michelle Williams stars.

★ *Courageous* (2011, PG-13, violence): Christian film about four police officers forming a sort of alliance to bolster their faith and help each other be better husbands/fathers. Overlong but involving examination of parental responsibility and personal integrity in the face of tragedy and everyday stress. Not graphic, but pulls no punches as police deal with gangs and drugs.

★ *Mao's Last Dancer* (2010, PG, some violence, language): This stirring Australian film is the true story of a Chinese ballet dancer (performed wonderfully by Chai Cao) who defects in the late 1970s to dance with the Houston Ballet, then with the Australian Ballet.

★ *Extraordinary Measures* (2010, PG, profanity): A couple (Brendan Fraser, Keri Russell) whose two children have a rare condition that causes death by age 10, align themselves with a cantankerous medical researcher (Harrison Ford) to race for a cure. True story of how prickly personalities and corporate profit margins can derail disease research.

★ *The Great Buck Howard* (2009, PG, mild language): A law student (Colin Hanks) drops out to become road manager for a has-been mentalist (based loosely on real-life mentalist The Amazing Kreskin) in this comedy-drama about the downhill slope of show business for late-in-life minor celebrities. Lots of star cameos, including Hanks' dad, Tom.

Johnny Depp and Kate Winslet in Marc Forster's Finding Neverland *(2004) — Miramax*

★ *No Reservations* (2007, PG, some profanity, mild sexual innuendo): An upscale workaholic chef (Catherine Zeta-Jones) unexpectedly gains custody of her young niece while feeling threatened by a new sous chef (Aaron Eckhart). Gentle romantic comedy.

★ *The Ultimate Gift* (2007, PG, some violence and profanity): When a wealthy magnate (James Garner) dies, he leaves his estate to his spoiled playboy grandson (Drew Fuller), but only if he performs certain tasks designed to make him a better person. Sentimental but effective Christian drama.

★ *The Astronaut Farmer* (2007, PG, profanity): Billy Bob Thornton is a farmer with a degree in astrophysics and a rocket in his barn, and when he decides to launch himself into outer space, the FBI takes an unnerving interest. Offbeat fable about a dreamer at odds with our post-911 world.

★ *Miss Potter* (2006, PG, should be rated G): Comedy mixes with tragedy in this excellent biography of Victorian author/watercolorist Beatrix Potter (Renee Zellweger) and the publisher who became the love of her life, Norman Warne (Ewan McGregor).

★ *Finding Neverland* (2004, PG, mild profanity): Johnny Depp is J.M. Barrie, whose relationship with a widowed neighbor (Kate Winslet) and her sons inspires him to write *Peter Pan*. Wonderfully performed tender story with notable cinematography.

★ *The Dish* (2000, PG-13, profanity, including the f-word once, vulgarity): Funny and warm true story of quirky characters in a small Australia farming community where a satellite dish in a sheep-farm meadow is NASA's backup to track the Apollo XI space mission in 1969.

★ *Return to Me* (2000, PG, some profanity): Excellent, gentle comedy-drama from filmmaker Bonnie Hunt, who also co-stars in story of a heart transplant recipient (Minnie Driver) who falls for a widower (David Duchnovy), unaware that they have a vital connection.

SPORTS/COMPETITION

★ *The Mighty Macs* (2011, G): Carla Gugino stars as a real-life, ahead-of-her-time women's basketball coach at a Catholic college in the early 1970s, butting heads with Ellen Burstyn as the Reverend Mother.

★ *Seven Days in Utopia* (2011, G): After blowing his professional debut with a very public meltdown, a young golf prodigy (Lucas Black) finds redemption in a small Texas town with help from a retired pro (Robert Duvall). This Christian film is loaded with clichés, but Duvall makes it easy to take.

★ *Soul Surfer* (2011, PG, violent shark attack): Tremendously moving true story of a young teenage surfer who loses an arm to a shark, then, after working through her anger and grief, and relying on her Christian faith, manages to relearn how to use a board and ultimately returns to surfing competiton.

★ *Secretariat* (2010, PG, very mild profanity; could be rated G): True story of 1970s Denver housewife (Diane Lane) who reluctantly takes over her father's Virginia stables and with an eccentric trainer (John Malkovich) manages to fight through the chauvinistic racing industry to turn the title horse into the first Triple Crown winner in twenty-five years. Engrossing, exciting, and often very funny.

★ *Invictus* (2009, PG-13, if not for two utterances of the f-word this could easily be rated PG for sports violence): Newly elected South African president Nelson Mandela (Morgan Freeman in peak form) attempts to unite black and white by motivating a rugby team to go for the World Cup. Remarkable true story co-stars Matt Damon as the rugby star that helps him do it.

★ *Leatherheads* (2008, PG-13, profanity, football violence): Funny, old-fashioned rowdy comedy set in 1925 during the early days of football as George Clooney recruits a World War I hero (John Krasinski) while a reporter (Renee Zellweger) digs for proof that he's a fraud.

★ *Pride* (2007, PG, some violence and profanity): Fine true story of swim coach James Ellis (Terrence Howard) motivating inner-city teens in the 1970s.

★ *We Are Marshall* (2006, PG, aftermath of a plane crash, football violence, some language): Gripping dramatization of the rebuilding of the Marshall University football team after a 1970 plane crash killed thirty-seven players, along with coaches, trainers, and boosters. Matthew McConaughey stars.

★ *Akeelah and the Bee* (2006, PG, mild profanity): Sharp, funny, and warm story of a young girl (luminous Keke Palmer) with an amazing knack for memorizing words who finds herself on track for the National Spelling Bee, despite lacking self-confidence.

★ *Invincible* (2006, PG, football violence, mild profanity): Another true story about an everyday guy up against impossible odds, this one about bartender Vince Papale (Mark Wahlberg) who goes to open tryouts for the Philadelphia Eagles and, to his surprise, makes the team.

★ *Glory Road* (2006, PG, mild language and violence): Rousing true story of Texas Western College coach Don Haskins (Josh Lucas), who recruited inner-city youth for his basketball team, which became the first with an all-black starting lineup in NCAA history.

★ *The World's Fastest Indian* (2005, PG-13, profanity, implied sex): The title refers to a 1920 motorcycle in this funny and thrilling true story of sixty-something New Zealander Burt Munro (Anthony Hopkins) who travels to the United States in the late 1960s to race his rattletrap bike on the Bonneville Salt Flats and manages to set a land speed record that has yet to be broken.

★ *The Greatest Game Ever Played* (2005, PG, mild language, violence): Entertaining biographical film with something to say about class prejudices tells the story of young Francis Quimet (Shia LeBeouf) who overcame the odds to become a golf champion in the early 20th century.

★ *Bobby Jones: Stroke of Genius* (2004, PG, some profanity): Superficial, but interesting look at the life of golf champion Bobby Jones (Jim Caviezel), who won the Grand Slam in 1930—all four major tournaments of the era in a single year.

★ *Miracle* (2004, PG, violence, profanity): Even though we all know the outcome of the amazing U.S. hockey team victory at the 1980 Winter Olympics, it's impossible not to get caught up in this excellent retelling. Kurt Russell stars.

★ *The Rookie* (2002, G): Dennis Quaid is terrific as real-life fastball pitcher Jim Morris, who won a brief but notable career in Major League Baseball at age thirty-five.

★ *Remember the Titans* (2000, PG, violence, language): Denzel Washington is great in this true story of forced integration in 1971 Virginia as a beleaguered high school football coach striving to help his players overcome differences and become a team. Predictable, but effective storytelling.

MOVIES FROM THE 1990s

FOR FAMILIES

★ *Mr. Holland's Opus* (1996, PG, profanity): Beginning in the 1960s, three decades of a dedicated music teacher's interaction with students are on display as Disney updates *Goodbye, Mr. Chips*. Sentimental to be sure, but Richard Dreyfuss' superb performance keeps it on track.

★ *Fly Away Home* (1996, PG, car crash, mild language): When her mother is killed, a girl (Anna Paquin) moves back in with her neglectful father (Jeff Daniels), but when some wild geese bond with her, father and daughter work together to help them re-create their migration pattern. Uneven, but stunning final third makes up for weaknesses in based-on-fact story.

★ *Squanto: A Warrior's Tale* (1994, PG): In the early 17th century, an American Indian (Adam Beach) is captured and taken to England as a sort of sideshow attraction, but he escapes and attempts to make his way back home. Very loosely based on the real Squanto, this Disney adventure is over the top, but enjoyable.

★ *The Secret of Roan Inish* (1994, PG): Captivating, lyrical Irish fable (from American independent filmmaker John Sayles) set in small village after World War II as a young girl living with her grandparents finds evidence of real, live selkies, mythological half-human/half-seal creatures.

★ *Groundhog Day* (1993, PG, comic suicide attempts, discreet sexual innuendo, mild language): *The Twilight Zone* meets Frank Capra as an arrogant weatherman (Bill Murray) becomes a better person after having to literally live the same day over and over again. Very funny, insightful comedy with terrific performances from all concerned.

★ *Matinee* (1993, PG, campy violence, mild language): Zany nostalgic comedy set against the backdrop of the Cuban missile crisis in 1962 Key West, Fla., has a familiar coming-of-age story at its center, but it's at its best—and funniest—when focusing on a genial low-budget filmmaker/showman (John Goodman) as he premieres his newest scary movie, *Mant*, about a mutant half-man, half-ant.

★ *Searching for Bobby Fischer* (1993, PG, should be G): You don't have to understand chess to revel in this first-rate true story of a seven-year-old chess prodigy (Max Pomeranc) whose parents (Joe Mantegna, Joan Allen) must ultimately decide whether to pursue tournaments or allow him a real childhood. Ben Kingsley and Laurence Fishburne are also excellent as completely different players who encourage the boy.

★ *Rudy* (1993, PG, football violence, foul language): True story of "Rudy" Ruettiger (Sean Astin) who overcomes his small stature, lack of discernible football skill, poor grades, and no money to achieve his dream of playing for Notre Dame. A real come-from-behind, follow-your-dreams story of the first order.

★ *Cool Runnings* (1993, PG, foul language): Funny, involving Disney film about four Jamaicans who want Olympic gold, so they form a bobsled team, though they've never seen a bobsled . . . or snow. John Candy is the down-and-out-coach who helps them succeed. And, believe it or not, it's true.

★ *A Home of Our Own* (1993, PG, mild language, violence): Kathy Bates is a strong-willed, angry-at-her-circumstances widow with six kids and no money who quixotically leaves Los Angeles and plants roots in rural Idaho.

Andie MacDowell and Bill Murray in Harold Ramis' Groundhog Day *(1993)*
—Columbia

★ *Father of the Bride/Father of the Bride, Part II* (1991/1995, PG, mild vulgarity): Two frothy remakes of 1950/1951 comedies with Steve Martin, this time as the father having trouble letting go of his about-to-be-married daughter, then being overwhelmed by the wedding preparations. Both films are basically showcases for Martin, but he gets help from Diane Keaton as his wife and comic supporting players.

★ *What About Bob?* (1991, PG, foul language): Psychiatrist Richard Dreyfuss takes his family to their New Hampshire summer home for a month, but everything-phobic patient Bill Murray tracks him down, endears himself to the family—and the entire town—while driving Dreyfuss crazy. Thin, but funny comedy with the stars giving it their all.

★ *White Fang* (1991, PG, violence, some language): Solid, epic-scale family adventure from Jack London's classic tale of a gold-hunter (Ethan Hawke) and the part-dog wolf he befriends. Beautifully photographed Alaskan wilderness backgrounds.

★ *Wild Hearts Can't Be Broken* (1991, G): Well-made, true story from Disney of Sonora Webster (Gabrielle Anwar), a young woman in the 1930s who runs off with a wild west show (operated by Cliff Robertson, looking for all the world like Buffalo Bill Cody) and learns to ride horses that dive from a thirty-foot tower into a pool of water.

FOR PARENTS

★ *The Straight Story* (1999, G): Wonderful character-driven true story of elderly Alvin Straight (Richard Farnsworth) riding 300 miles on his lawnmower to see his estranged brother.

★ *The Winslow Boy* (1999, G): Set in 1911 England, this adaptation of Terence Rattigan's play tells the compelling story of a young man booted out of the Royal Naval Academy when he's accused of theft, and his family's strenuous efforts to exonerate him.

★ *Runaway Bride* (1999, PG, foul language): Comedy reuniting the stars (Julia Roberts, Richard Gere) and director (Garry Marshall) of *Pretty Woman* has reporter Gere fired for not verifying facts in a column about Roberts, who has left three fiancés at the altar.

★ *The Spanish Prisoner* (1998, PG, mild violence, language): Low-key thriller starring Campbell Scott and, in an atypical straight role, Steve Martin, about characters mounting the elaborate con game of the title.

★ *Waking Ned Devine* (1998, PG, Discreet nudity of two elderly men, some foul language): Quirky populace of a tiny Irish village bands together to take advantage of a winning lottery ticket whose owner has died of shock. Very funny, distinctly British comedy.

★ *Mrs. Brown* (1997, PG, skinny-dipping men, mild language): In 1864, widowed Queen Victoria (Judi Dench) is finally pulled out of mourning by her late husband's rowdy horseman (Billy Connolly). Rich, detailed, beautifully photographed, and with two superb performances at its center.

★ *One Fine Day* (1996, PG, some profanity): Michelle Pfeiffer and George Clooney are harried single parents in Manhattan forced to rely on each other during one particularly hectic day. Sweet, funny romantic comedy that will resonate with parents.

★ *The Whole Wide World* (1996, PG, language, nude drawings): Small, delicate, beautifully realized film begins as comedy and ultimately ends in tragedy, telling the story of socially awkward Robert E. Howard (Vincent D'Onofrio), author of *Conan the Barbarian* stories in pulp magazines, and independent schoolteacher/aspiring writer Novalyne Price (Renee Zellweger) in 1933 Texas.

★ *The Grass Harp* (1996, PG, mild language): Easygoing comedy-drama set in the 1940s has an orphaned boy (Edward Furlong) taken in by his eccentric aunts (Piper Laurie, Sissy Spacek). An expert cast—including Walter Matthau, Jack Lemmon, and Mary Steenburgen—creates an array of fine-tuned characters.

★ *Once Upon a Time . . . When We Were Colored* (1996, PG, mild violence and language): Episodic but affecting story of an impoverished black community in Mississippi, primarily focusing on one boy's maturation against the backdrop of changes in the rural South between 1946 and 1962. Terrific cast led by Al Freeman Jr., Phylicia Rashad, and Richard Roundtree.

★ *Emma* (1996, should be G): Funny adaptation of the Jane Austen novel about the busiest of busybodies (Gwyneth Paltrow) and her self-absorbed, if misguided matchmaking efforts. Great cast includes Ewan McGregor, Toni Collette, and Jeremy Northam.

★ *Unstrung Heroes* (1995, PG, some language): Touching, offbeat comedy-drama about a young boy in the 1960s trying to cope with a mother dying of cancer (Andie MacDowell) and a father in denial (John Turturro), so he moves in with two extremely eccentric uncles and tries to find his own way.

★ *Sense and Sensibility* (1995, PG, should be G): Spirited, engaging comedy-drama from the Jane Austen story of very different sisters (Emma Thompson, Kate Winslet) and their rocky roads to romance in early 19th century England. Great cast includes Hugh Grant and Alan Rickman. Thompson also wrote the Oscar-winning screenplay.

★ *Sabrina* (1995, PG, mild profanity): Remake of the 1954 romantic-comedy classic stands up well thanks to the charms of Harrison Ford, Greg Kinnear, and Julia Ormond in story of chauffeur's daughter wooed by two wealthy brothers—a buttoned-down businessman and a carefree playboy.

★ *Little Women* (1994, PG, should be G): Wonderful realization of Louisa May Alcott's novel nicely balances comedy and drama in story of four sisters growing up during the Civil War, with a great cast of stars (Susan Sarandon, Winona Ryder) and future stars (Claire Danes, Kirstin Dunst, Christian Bale). Veteran character actress Mary Wickes nearly steals the show.

★ *It Could Happen to You* (1994, PG, mild violence, language): Nicolas Cage and Bridget Fonda are most appealing in this gentle comedy that spins off the true story of a cop that gave half his lottery ticket to a waitress for a tip, and they won. So Cage and Fonda start giving it away, even as his materialistic wife (Rosie Perez) starts spending it as fast as she can.

★ *I.Q.* (1994, PG. mild language): Delightfully sunny comedy set in the 1950s about an auto mechanic (Tim Robbins) with eyes for the ditsy, but mathematically brilliant niece (Meg Ryan) of none other than Albert Einstein

(Walter Matthau). Filled with wonderful characters and warm, but often hilarious, humor.

★ *The Hudsucker Proxy* (1994, PG, mild language, comic suicide): Broad, 1950s-era Frank Capra-style fantasy-comedy has bumpkin Tim Robbins arriving in Manhattan just in time to be made a patsy by Paul Newman for a company in crisis. A definite change of pace for the usually much darker Coen brothers.

★ *Shadowlands* (1993, PG, should be G): Low-key, but involving true story set in the 1950s about confirmed bachelor C.S. Lewis (Anthony Hopkins) finding unlikely romance late in life with a feisty American poet, Joy Gresham (Debra Winger). The stars are great in one of director Richard Attenborough's best films.

★ *The Remains of the Day* (1993, PG, should be G): Anthony Hopkins and Emma Thompson are quite amazing in this very low-key but intriguing story of a repressed butler who just can't declare his feelings for a warm-hearted housekeeper in pre-World War II England. Christopher Reeve has a nice supporting role.

★ *The Age of Innocence* (1993, PG, mild language, nude art): An unlikely choice for director Martin Scorsese, this adaptation of Edith Wharton's novel of star-crossed love in cloistered 1870s high society is rich in character and mood, with fine performances from Daniel Day-Lewis, Michelle Pfeiffer, and Winona Ryder.

★ *Howards End* (1992, PG, mild language, violence): A gripping treatise on how the people with whom we interact can affect us for good and ill in the story of three families whose lives intersect in unexpected ways. Wonderfully performed by Emma Thompson, Anthony Hopkins, and Helena Bonham Carter, among others.

★ *Enchanted April* (1992, PG, should be G): "Enchanted" is right. This low-key, English period comedy has four disparate women pooling resources to leave wet and dreary London and rent an Italian castle for a month, finding it has an intoxicating effect on all who visit. Completely winning with a wonderful cast.

★ *Defending Your Life* (1991, PG, mild language, innuendo): Albert Brooks wrote, directed, and stars with Meryl Streep in this hilarious view of the afterlife, with something to say about facing our fears.

★ *The Doctor* (1991, PG-13, some foul language, hospital gore): Excellent story of a cold, aloof, but respected cardiovascular surgeon (William Hurt) who begins to see things differently after being diagnosed with throat cancer and finding himself subjected to the same indignities he has foisted on patients for years.

★ *Avalon* (1990, PG, very mild profanity): Utterly delightful multi-generational story covering fifty years in the lives of a loving family in Baltimore beginning with the patriarch's immigration from Eastern Europe in 1914.

★ *Awakenings* (1990, PG-13, mild violence, profanity, including one f-word): Robin Williams shines in this true story of a shy physician in the 1960s whose work with near comatose patients brought remarkable, if short-lived results. Robert De Niro is the first patient brought back to "life" after 30 years of being unable to do anything for himself.

★ *Joe Versus the Volcano* (1990, PG, a few profanities): Quirky, zany, funny tale of a worn-down worker (Tom Hanks) with six months to live taking up a millionaire's offer to help him live his last days in high style if he'll jump into a volcano to appease some natives so that they'll sell their mineral rights. Meg Ryan steals the show playing three very different characters.

Afterword

THE FUTURE OF MOVIES

Is Not All Downhill

It will probably not surprise you to learn that I have grandkids that have taken an interest in cinema and are taking film classes, both at the high school and college levels. And it's interesting to hear them talk about the movies their instructors have chosen to show them, and how they feel about these older pictures.

Two of my high school-age grandsons saw movies that are considered timeless classics by film buffs and national critics, but they were not so impressed. Jonah said he "had to watch *Casablanca*," saying it as if he had been forced to swallow castor oil . . . which, come to think of it, is another antiquated comparison that shows my age. Anyway, he said he found it quite boring.

Discussing a few specific sequences, he conceded that, yeah, that part was funny, and yeah, this bit was OK, but his view didn't change. "It was still boring," he said, as if I had misinterpreted the first time he said so.

Meanwhile, his brother Adam watched *Citizen Kane* and thought it was "weird, but interesting." That was about all he could muster.

Hey, they're kids. I'll check back with them in ten years.

In a way, their exposure to these movies is aesthetically worse than when I saw them for the first time in the early 1960s on a small black-and-white TV screen with commercial interruptions every ten or fifteen minutes. In these high school classes, they are surrounded by kids who are even less interested than they are, with hour-long periods that force the instructors to break up the films into sections over two or three periods, sometimes days apart. That's hardly the best way to view either one—but especially *Citizen Kane*, which jumps around in time with flashbacks.

But, I'm not complaining. That's just the nature of high school.

South African born British actor Basil Rathbone portrayed Sir Arthur Conan Doyle's detective Sherlock Holmes in fourteen films between 1939 and 1946. —Universal

And, frankly, I'm glad they're being exposed to them at all. I doubt that I would be able to get them to sit and watch one of them with me, unless I was willing to endure *Mystery Science Theater 3000/Riff-Trax*-style snarky comments from beginning to end.

Another grandson, Connor, who is studying film in college said his class is in a theater setting, one day a week for a four-hour session. So the class members watch a movie with plenty of time left for discussion, a much better way to appreciate the experience. And because he's older, he's a little more open to new motion-picture experiences. Coming up, he explained, is an old Sherlock Holmes movie. His instructor "let us know it wasn't the Robert Downey Jr. version," he said with a laugh. I thought about telling him how much I prefer Basil Rathbone, but that wouldn't mean anything to him at this point.

When I was a kid I kept up with new movies, but I also loved old movies so much that my father was baffled by my level of interest, especially since it covered all genres, including two for which he had no use; documentaries and foreign films. "Where does that come from?" he'd ask from time to time. And when I went through a period of reading books about silent movies, few of which I was able to see at that point, he took to telling people that I was forty years old when I was born.

Perhaps, I was unwittingly preparing for my later movie-reviewing career, since to do it right you have to be open to every genre and every era. But in my youth, actually seeing the classic movies I had read about was strictly catch as catch can. I remember when, against their better judgment, my parents let me stay up on a weeknight to watch a 1 a.m. showing of *Citizen Kane* on a local channel. I saw maybe five minutes before falling into a deep sleep. I was very frustrated with myself, and it was a few years before I was able to catch up with it again. That's a lot different than simply calling up your Netflix queue and watching it at your leisure.

Of course, it's only natural that, despite the availability of so many movies new and old and the vast array of opportunities and venues to view them, young people tend to stick with what they know, their favorite movies as old as two years ago. Hence, the many sequels, remakes, and spinoffs that all resemble each other and dominate theaters so that it seems there's always a relative lack of variety in what's playing.

And while many younger audience members seem to have acclimated to modern cinematic styles, I continue to find some of them annoying, especially nausea-inducing shaky-camera techniques and cinematography that mutes colors in favor of bleached-out muddy skylines or steely gray panoramas . . . I really don't understand why filmmakers favor such things. Can't we buy them tripods and convince them that the world is not a dingy brown?

Similarly, the proliferation of graphic sexual content and coarse language in so many movies, especially comedies, has caused my wife and I to comment from time to time how sad we are that there are so few comic films, especially light romances, that we are comfortable sitting through.

I know all of this makes me sound terribly old, and these days, well, I guess I am. But I've actually been writing/complaining about such things since I was in my late twenties. So, perhaps I'm an old soul. On the other hand, if I was forty at birth, then I was really eighty when I was twenty. So perhaps, I've just always been old.

Still, there seems to be, among some at least, a thirst for better, cleaner material. How else does one explain the sudden explosion in 2012 of digitally remastered vintage movies thriving with one-day (and occasional one-week) screenings all over the country?

The national Cinemark Theatre chain and Fathom Events (sometimes in conjunction with Turner Classic Movies) have been offering all across the country simultaneous one-day showings of such films as *Singin' in the Rain*, *Jaws*, *North By Northwest*, *Doctor Zhivago*, *Lawrence of Arabia*, *E.T.: The Extra-Terrestrial*, *The Birds* and the Halloween double-bill *Frankenstein* and *Bride of Frankenstein*—yes, the old black-and-white Boris Karloff films from the early 1930s.

Check out upcoming films in your area at these links:

★ Cinemark: www.cinemark.com/cinemark-classic-series

★ Fathom: www.fathomevents.com

★ Turner Classic Movies: www.tcm.com

When my wife and I have attended these, there have certainly been many of our gray- and white-haired peers sitting around us, but there have also been a lot of young people, including teens and preteens. And while some of these screenings have been fairly empty, others have been surprisingly well-attended. *Singin' in the Rain* nearly sold out the 300-seat auditorium attended by my family (eighteen of us, including kids and grandkids), and that one-night screening apparently did well all around the country since it returned for an encore two months later.

Omar Sharif and Peter O'Toole in David Lean's* Lawrence of Arabia *(1962) — Columbia

And there have been others. A major multiplex in my town played *To Kill a Mockingbird* for a week in April 2012, and there was a week-long national release of *Raiders of the Lost Ark* in September after it had been reconfigured for exclusive IMAX showings. And many cities around the country have repertory movie houses that frequently cycle through older titles.

Of course, I realize that none of these special screenings of older movies is ever going to really compete with the blockbusters at your local multiplex. But the fact that there are moviegoers out there willing to purchase tickets to see them in a darkened theater—when they could easily rent and watch them at home for a dollar or two—says to me that there is still an audience that would like to go to the movies and be carried away for a couple of hours without feeling insulted or pummeled or offended or uncomfortable.

Having said all this, I do live in the real world, and I know that Pandora's Box has been opened. Hollywood is never going to clean up its act and movies will never go back to what they once were. But, we can hope all the same that filmmakers and studios don't blanch if their movies get softer ratings and race to insert something vulgar to ensure a PG-13. Trust me, if *Avengers 2* were to come in with a G or PG, it would in no way diminish its box-office take. That's not going to happen, but you get my meaning.

Modern moviemakers can still tell relevant stories with which everyday people can identify, and do so in a way that isn't in your face or aggressively vulgar, as shown by the many films listed in Chapter 10.

Obviously, there are still filmmakers out there willing and able to make those kinds of movies. At least so long as they prove to be profitable. So, let's help make them profitable.

Index of Films

ABOUT THE PUBLISHER

Familius was founded in 2012 with the intent to align the founders' love of publishing and family with the digital publishing renaissance which occurred simultaneously with the Great Recession. The founders believe that the traditional family is the basic unit of society, and that a society is only as strong as the families that create it.

Familius' mission is to help families be happy. We invite you to participate with us in strengthening your family by being part of the Familius family. Go to www.familius.com to subscribe and receive information about our books, articles, and videos.

Website: www.familius.com
Facebook: www.facebook.com/paterfamilius
Twitter: @paterfamilius1 and @familiustalk
Pinterest: www.pinterest.com/familius

familius

CPSIA information can be obtained at www.ICGtesting.com
Printed in the USA
BVOW010828040313

314371BV00006B/11/P

9 781938 301193